More praise for *Closing the Leadership Gap:*

"Marie Wilson is a revolutionary thinker who has brought her passion and experience to give a clear picture of where we really are and how far we still need to come."

—Billie Jean King

"You won't find a stronger set of arguments for making sure more women reach the top. Marie Wilson focuses her passion and her scholarship on the stunning scarcity of American women in leadership positions, even as we move full speed into the twenty-first century. She provides hard evidence our country will suffer unless we do something about it."

—Judy Woodruff, Senior Correspondent and Prime Anchor, CNN

"I am thrilled that Marie Wilson is tackling such an important issue in *Closing the Leadership Gap* and believe her efforts to promote women as relevant and vital contributors to all aspects of society will make a meaningful difference for years to come."

—Mellody Hobson, President, Ariel Capital Management, Inc.

"Marie Wilson draws a bead on the challenges women everywhere face as they take on leadership roles—must reading for every woman who aspires to lead and a valuable guide for anyone who wants to upset the status quo."

—Wendy D. Puriefoy, President, Public Education Network

"I loved reading this leadership book. It focuses attention on the enormous untapped potential of women to lead this country and their community, both politically and economically."

—Lt. General Claudia J. Kennedy (Ret.), first female three-star general in the U.S. Army

"Marie Wilson reminds us that all women can use the power of culture to create opportunity and make our voices heard in order to better the nation and the world."

——House Democratic Leader Nancy Pelosi

CLOSING THE LEADERSHIP GAP

CLOSING THE LEADERSHIP GAP

WHY WOMEN CAN AND MUST HELP RUN THE WORLD

Marie C. Wilson

VIKING

For my mother, who trusts me
And for Nancy, who teaches me to trust myself

VIKING
Published by the Penguin Group
Penguin Group (USA) Inc., 375 Hudson Street,
New York, New York 10014, U.S.A.
Penguin Books Ltd, 80 Strand,
London WC2R 0RL, England
Penguin Books Australia Ltd, 250 Camberwell Road, Camberwell,
Victoria 3124, Australia
Penguin Books Canada Ltd, 10 Alcorn Avenue,
Toronto, Ontario, Canada M4V 3B2
Penguin Books India (P) Ltd, 11 Community Centre, Panchsheel Park,
New Delhi–110 017, India
Penguin Books (N.Z.) Ltd, Cnr Rosedale and Airborne Roads, Albany,
Auckland, New Zealand
Penguin Books (South Africa) (Pty) Ltd, 24 Sturdee Avenue,
Rosebank, Johannesburg 2196, South Africa

Penguin Books Ltd, Registered Offices:
80 Strand, London WC2R 0RL, England

First published in 2004 by Viking Penguin,
a member of Penguin Group (USA) Inc.

10 9 8 7 6 5 4 3 2 1

Library of Congress Cataloging-in-Publication Data

Wilson, Marie (Marie C.)
  Closing the leadership gap / Marie C. Wilson.
    p.   cm.
  Includes bibliographical references and index.
  ISBN 0-670-03274-3
    1. Leadership. 2. Businesswomen. I. Title.

  HD57.7.W544 2004
  658.4'092'082—dc22   2003065770

This book is printed on acid-free paper. ∞

Printed in the United States of America
Set in Bembo
Designed by Erin Benach

Contents

Introduction: It's About Time   ix

1. Why Women Matter   1

2. Barriers to Leadership   17

3. Authority   33

4. Ambition   53

5. Ability   71

6. Authenticity   95

7. Culture   117

8. The Business of Transformation   137

9. Parting Words: The Voice of Experience   151

Acknowledgments   167

Notes   171

Bibliography   183

Index   187

INTRODUCTION: IT'S ABOUT TIME

All of my adult life I have preached the virtues of power sharing between men and women. The arrangement seemed not only fair, but also obvious: Women populate half the democracy; we should occupy half the positions of leadership—both for gender equity and because women, a natural resource, should be mined for energy.

Now when I think of women in leadership, I think of it not only as the fair thing to do, but also as the *only* thing to do. In a few short years the world has become very unstable. Terrorists attacked us on our soil; in response we waged war against Afghanistan and Iraq. The formerly robust U.S. economy will soon sag under the biggest deficit in its history. Corporate greed has wiped out whole companies along with hundreds of thousands of jobs. Millions of Americans continue to live without adequate health care.

When I look at the issues we face, and when I think of the changes we need, I am as convinced as I have ever been that our future depends on the leadership of women—not to replace men, but to transform our options alongside them.

● ● ●

I grew up in the 1940s and 1950s, when women were truly limited to a supporting role. I was Homecoming Queen and a class officer (but not the president). I was a cheerleader. I won beauty contests in my hometown of Atlanta. I married poor but with promise, then nearly went mad in the isolation of a small apartment with a baby. Through the years, while minding a growing family and the household chores, I finished my B.A. in philosophy and my master's degree in education.

My first professional job (I had been a church volunteer and had worked in the civil rights movement) was at Drake University as director of women's programs. To help women like me, I crafted economic development programs, job shares, and training for female "retreads" reentering the workforce after raising a family. These concepts are accepted today, but in the 1970s they were considered edgy.

I left Drake to make more money for our family of five children, several of whom were approaching college age. My experience as a social entrepreneur landed me an executive position in education and human resources with business entrepreneurs—men who were instrumental in creating the first cash machines in America. It seemed a natural fit, but it wasn't. This banking association reflected the more conservative banking community it served. My modest efforts to modernize their views of women were considered dangerous and revolutionary. They probably would have fired me if my division hadn't been making money.

If you strip away the particulars, I have led an American woman's life—running a complicated household, doing what I had to do to financially support the family, managing the home while bringing in a paycheck, and suppressing screams as my ideas were trivialized in the workplace.

It only made me trust women all the more, which was why I couldn't resist the dare of a friend to apply for the job of executive director at the Ms. Foundation for Women in New York City. I doubted those easterners would consider hiring a midwestern woman with southern roots. I was wrong. So in the mid 1980s, I left both a newly won city council seat and the banking job to run the foundation (best known for a program we created in 1993, Take Our Daughters to Work). Finally, I had found my fit, and I helped build one of the largest women's foundations in America.

At the Ms. Foundation we are social entrepreneurs with a practical eye on today and a vision for tomorrow. We take on issues that directly affect women's lives—economic development, safety, and reproductive health, for instance—which is why we knew we had to have substantial numbers of women at the top in America to help women at all levels. We saw what happened when we *didn't*. Hence, the White House Project, whose mission is to advance women's leadership in every sector, up to and including the presidency, changing society from a system built on the labor of women to one led equally by their vision.

Never has this been more necessary than now, when so many issues are *our* issues: education, health and elder care, and violence in all forms. In the past these concerns have been marginalized because of their connection to women; today, they are on everyone's agenda. And though war may not be our traditional battleground, it is the arena where women are needed most, to make and maintain the peace.

Men *and* women must be in power to moderate the influence of masculinity on all of us. It is this power sharing that will provide a different voice at the table, giving women the opportunity to shape policy in line with our values and giving men any permission they need to bring all of themselves to leadership, including their softer side.

Right now, for all its strides, our country is tremendously imbalanced in gender leadership. Of 435 seats in the House of Representatives, only 59 are occupied by women; of 100 senators, only 14 are women. Only 24 women have ever been governors in the United States. Women are nearly half the workforce, yet we make up only 12 percent of top executives and 15.7 percent of corporate officers; we hold a mere 12.4 percent of board seats in five hundred of the country's largest companies.

Internationally, the United States ranks sixtieth in women's political leadership, behind Sierra Leone and tied with Andorra. Even in so-called third world countries like India, huge strides have been made to bring women into power. Norway, whose parliament is 36.4 percent women, will vote soon on proposed legislation that would make the boards of every publicly traded company include at least 40 percent women by 2005. Yet here at home, despite the enormous gains we have made in the last twenty-five years, the "cultural ideal" for a woman remains that of wife and mother.

If you find this as hard to believe as I do, just look at the snail's pace of structural change that would allow women and men to fully integrate work and family. Women routinely work outside the home (mostly in low-paying jobs), yet we are still expected to be the primary caregivers, responsible for everything domestic. I truly believe that if we install enough women in leadership, they will create new policies for old institutions, shifting the burden from one set of shoulders to many, allowing women (and men) to be good parents and great leaders. And women will add their own recipe of strong values—inclusion, communication across lines of authority, the work of caring, relationship building—all of which would increase satisfaction and productivity everywhere.

But how do we get there? That's what this book is about.

It is not a scholarly work and it is not comprehensive; it is a book about experience—*my* experience and the lessons I've learned—backed by research conducted and gathered at the White House Project and the Ms. Foundation. It is a book of stories and facts, historical and current, with suggestions for how we might all, in our own way, put more women at the top, possibly even ourselves. If empirical data and hands-on experience have taught me anything, it is this: Change must be sweeping, and it won't be easy. When it comes to women's leadership, we live in a land of deep resistance, with structural and emotional impediments burned into the cultures of our organizations, into our society, and into the psyches and expectations of both sexes. The problem is layered, as is the solution.

That's why *numbers matter.* A single woman leader or a few women in a larger group are tokens; each token has to prove she's man enough for the job. We saw it played out in the seventies, as America began to deal with gender and race in the workplace. Women and minorities were scattered throughout corporations at the time—one here and one there, isolated as stereotypes, often unable to speak their minds unless they agreed with the dominant conclusion. How in the world could anyone fit in under these circumstances? Often we didn't, and it was used as proof that we shouldn't be in power. As the *first* and *only* in the workplace, we were objects of suspicion and derision.

Until there are enough diverse females in authority so that a chosen few are not expected to speak for an entire race or gender, those few will continue to carry the burden for us all. It is a fact that the more people like *you* in a working group, the more likely *you* are to be yourself. In a 2003 interview with Judy Woodruff of CNN, Associate Justice Sandra Day O'Connor, the first woman on the U.S. Supreme Court, described how she felt when Ruth Bader Ginsberg joined her on the bench: "The minute Justice Ginsberg came to the court, we were nine justices. It wasn't seven and then 'the women.' We became nine. And it was a great relief to me . . ."

But it is not just numbers. We also need strong civic and cultural organizations filled with women who will support their leaders—and hold them accountable. If ever we doubted that *critical mass* plus strong *civic engagement* equal lasting change, the women of South Africa put it to rest. They fought side by side with men to defeat apartheid, yet found themselves denied power once it was obtained in 1994. The women were simply not going to stand for it. They banded together their women's organizations and demanded a share of the leadership. Result: The African National Congress guaranteed women 30 percent of party seats. South Africa has moved from 141st to 15th in the world in women's political representation, with excellent legislation to show for it.

Negotiating a *new deal* enabling women to lead outside the home will require a new political will. We will have to reshape our country's institutions, making the environment hospitable both to women's leadership and men's blossoming domestic involvement. Imagine if America copied Norway and demanded that 40 percent of board seats in publicly funded companies be filled by women. Would we be struggling with the issues of child care or paid family medical leave? Not likely. We need to move our circles of life, public and private, into greater overlap to create one continuous community, allowing work and family to intersect the way they naturally would if our society hadn't forced them apart.

Cultural shifts require an organized effort and a woman-by-woman guerrilla campaign if we are to see change, especially as it relates to how women are represented in the media. The media provide what they think we want, which then translates to advertising and subscription dollars for their corporations. Through our buying power and our voices, we must demonstrate what we will and will not accept. We'll also occasionally need to go where no woman has gone before. For instance, I nearly lost my feminist credentials when I joined with Mattel to create a new Barbie doll. It was a case of invading the culture rather than fighting it, and using the tools of the culture to teach valuable lessons about democracy. Mattel eventually manufactured President Barbie in 2000 in several ethnicities. (But I couldn't convince them to make her shoes flat so she could stand on her own two feet.)

Culture is crucial to change because it provides role models (fictitious though some might be) for the world's power structure. We must work our way inside, even if it seems impossible, and demand that women be shown in top leadership positions. A good start would be a woman successor to Martin Sheen after he serves two terms as the president on *The West Wing*.

How quickly we get to critical mass also depends on changing the *perception* of women as leaders, and on starting to *value* female qualities rather than using them as an excuse to marginalize us as "work moms." In each of the following chapters, you will learn how, through guts and gumption, women have managed to outsmart the limits of our prescribed roles, providing a template for change. If enough of us follow their examples (and create our own methods of resistance), we will accelerate the movement of women into top positions.

Whenever the idea of women in leadership surfaces, one question is always asked: Will women change power or will power change women? Will women act just like men when they finally get the same opportunities? The answers are complicated. Yes, we will learn to lead like men if we are surrounded only by men; with little chance of speaking in a different and authentic voice, we will tend to join the pack. But we can and will become leaders honest to our values if we have enough support from other women and from like-minded men. Ultimately we will stand up and stand out.

Others already have. Great women, amazing women sit at the top of industry and politics, fighting the good fight. It is not as if we are starting from scratch, but as we will see from the statistics, these dynamic women are largely alone, functioning in an alien system. We must increase their numbers, give them sisters who can speak with voices aligned with their values, voices that are never lowered as they challenge the status quo and put forward unique ideas. Maybe these sisters are your sisters, or your daughters, or your best friends and mothers—or you.

But what if you don't want to be the president of the United States, or even the president of the PTA? You don't have to have a formal title to be a leader. You can stand up for yourself at work, or at the dinner table. You can volunteer for civic duty without running the show. You can write a letter to a network or to Congress, you can refuse to watch certain movies, and you can urge others to do the same. If you lead in your own life, you'll become a wave in the sea change.

▲▲▲

Over and over, as I wondered why I felt so driven to write this book, I found myself asking, What does it mean to trust women in a country that doesn't? I revisited hundreds of polls and press clips and studies and interviews; I rehashed the points of strength and weakness in my activism; I talked to friends and family, colleagues and leaders. The deeper my research, the clearer the answer: To trust women is to trust in a different future awash with ideas and lit by the energy of *all* people. It means more options. It means a fairer equation. It means the work of running the planet will be easier and better for all. If we don't do it for ourselves, we should certainly do it for our daughters, who have been led to believe—by us—that there are no limits. We should also do it for our sons, whose lives are severely limited by the accepted image of what it means to be boys and men.

We are at a tipping point as the world spins in complexity searching for solutions. John Naisbitt, author of *Megatrends,* tells the story of the American railroads, which faded because they did not ask, "What business are we in?" They failed to see they were no longer in the railroad business but, instead, in the transportation business. If we ask a similar question, we would answer that our business is no longer just gender equity, but the more sweeping industry of societal transformation. We *can* change old habits; we *can* find new ways of doing business. We can and *must* mobilize to do so, each in his or her own way.

▲ ▲ ▲

I became a leader through creativity, energy, and a little craziness. I certainly could never have imagined, from the viewpoint of that beauty queen in the fifties, that I would be where I am today. Nothing in the movies I loved or the women I admired showed me this was possible.

One old English expression describes courage as speaking your mind by telling all your heart. In the end, that is the other purpose of this book: not only to speak my heart, but also to suggest a world in which women *and* men are allowed to speak theirs. In that way, the cycle of change will be complete. Or, in the words of my colleague Laura Liswood of Harvard University's Council of Women World Leaders and a founder of the White House Project, it will move from "the unthinkable to the impossible to the inevitable."

1

WHY WOMEN MATTER

> When I first looked at this topic—why women
> matter and how women matter—I thought to
> myself, is this a question men would ask? I
> think not. They would ask, why does NATO
> matter, why does the UN matter, but they
> wouldn't ask why *they* matter.
>
> —*Laura Liswood, cofounder,
> Council of Women World Leaders,
> Harvard University*

October 1, 2002. *Fortune* magazine gathered the top leaders of the
female business elite into a packed auditorium of the New York
Stock Exchange. Powerful women—women who normally speak
alone at a podium—participated on panels at a summit to discuss issues that ranged from corporate governance to foreign policy.

Among the guests: Ann Moore, chair and CEO of Time Inc.;
Pat Mitchell, president and CEO of PBS; Andrea Jung, chair and
CEO of Avon Products, Inc.; tennis legend Billie Jean King; House
Democratic Leader Nancy Pelosi; Abby Joseph Cohen, managing
director of Goldman, Sachs & Co.; ABC correspondent and anchor
Barbara Walters; and actress and playwright Anna Deavere Smith.
Anna, who plays the president's national security adviser on *The West
Wing*, could watch her real-life counterpart, Condoleezza Rice, give
a keynote address that afternoon.

At a panel on leadership, former *Dateline NBC* anchor Jane

Pauley, the moderator, put a question to Anne M. Mulcahy, chair and CEO of Xerox Corporation: Do you think there's any significance to your being a woman?

Mulcahy's answer wound its way to no. The conversation bounced from Sherry Lansing, chair of Paramount Motion Picture Group, to Geraldine Ferraro, the first and only woman candidate to run for vice president of the United States from a major party. It became clear that these gifted leaders cared deeply about the progress of women, but few connected their gender directly to their work. "All of us are in this room because we are deserving," said Lansing.

Just six months before, at the same summit (postponed from September 2001 for obvious reasons), Carleton S. (Carly) Fiorina, chair and CEO of HP, created a stir when she denied there was a glass ceiling, saying women have to play by male rules and allow themselves to be judged by male standards, that if they don't, they risk being marginalized. (In July 2003, she modified that comment, telling an audience that she has faced barriers herself and knows they exist for others, but prefers not to focus on them.) Dinner conversation at the summit raged on both sides of the debate. At the end, during a radio show, women leaders disagreed with—and yet understood—Fiorina's point.

In the words of Anne Sweeney, president of ABC Cable Networks Group and president of the Disney Channel Worldwide: "I believe we will get to the point—God knows when it will be—when we will get to Carly's point [of having people be known] as the best in your field—period, amen—not man or woman." Marie J. Toulantis, CEO of Barnes & Noble.com: "There is not a woman I have ever spoken to in any position of authority in any company that will say [being a woman] has not made a difference, that they haven't had to be twice as smart as their male counterparts, have worked ten times harder, [waited] many years longer to get the [executive] position . . ." She also said, "I don't think it marginalizes women to say [we're different]; it recognizes we all have different styles. We are different than men and we should celebrate it."

● ● ●

Do we women lead differently? Yes, we do, whether from learned responses or lack of testosterone, and it is a hot underground topic for women at the top. "This is the great unspoken truth, the new orthodoxy that every woman I have encountered acknowledges—although usually only in private or with a group of other women," says author and businesswoman Margaret Heffernan in a 2002 *Fast Company* article. "Their caution betrays a fear that . . . acknowledgment of difference will come to mean an acceptance of inequality. A fear that 'different from' will morph into 'less than.'"

And so we find ourselves wedged into stereotypes, often acting against female values, trying to fit the male definition of leadership. It has come at a cost, but it has allowed us to slowly infiltrate the locker rooms of business and politics an inch at a time.

We are finally in the Senate on our own (without succeeding a deceased husband), and we govern states and cities. A woman has been nominated for vice president, and some have served in presidential cabinets. Madeleine K. Albright, the first female secretary of state, now heads an international group of three hundred women government ministers. We run Fortune 500 companies and large universities. We are among the fastest growth groups for entrepreneurship, with a woman starting a business every sixty seconds. Offices now experiment with alternative work arrangements. In the 1990s, the number of families with stay-at-home fathers and working mothers rose by 70 percent, resulting in nearly 2 million couples in reversals of traditional roles. *Working Mother* magazine goes beyond naming the 100 Best Companies for Women, now also naming the Best Companies for Women of Color.

You've come a long way, baby. Or have you? Let's look at those advances through a different filter.

Women are 51 percent of the U.S. population and 47 percent of the labor force, mostly in the lower rungs. Of workers making the minimum wage of $5.15 an hour or less, 63 percent are women. We also have a "second shift": More than 60 percent of us have jobs, but we're still responsible for domestic chores and child care in four out of five marriages.

Women may start a company a minute, but these businesses rarely reach scale, let alone achieve the "status of legend." If you take a couple of zeros off the Fortune 500, you have the approximate number of female CEOs amid them: Six. Parity on Fortune 500 board seats, if the current rate continues, will be reached in sixty years. We sit on 13.6 percent of the boards of the Fortune 500; at that rate, we will still occupy only 25 percent of the seats in twenty-five years. Women who are among the top five wage earners at their companies make 68 percent of the compensation of men doing the same job. Even in the world of nonprofits, where women are thought to be doing well, we see an enormous pay gap: Women at the top, on average, earn nearly $100,000 less than their male counterparts: $170,180 compared to men's $264,602.

We are only 14 percent of the present Congress, and it took us a long time to get there. Of nearly 12,000 people to serve in the legislature since the founding of the nation in 1776, only 215 (1.8 percent) have been women (and it is a very white world; the only black female ever elected to the Senate was Carol Moseley Braun, Democrat of Illinois). We are only 12 percent of both state governors and the mayors of the one hundred largest U.S. cities. Since the nation's founding, 582 people have served at the cabinet level under presidents; only 29 of them, or about 5 percent, have been women (the first being Secretary of Labor Frances Perkins under President Franklin D. Roosevelt from 1933 to 1945). Of those 29, two-thirds have served in the last decade, mostly in the administration of President Bill Clinton.

It gets worse at the state level, where the number of women in politics has been stagnant at about 20 percent for a decade. Since few U.S. presidents emerge from nowhere—they usually start in state feeder positions, then go national—the lack of women in the political pipeline is a serious issue for electing a woman to the highest office. Four of our last five presidents have been governors, and all of the last five vice presidents have served in Congress. At the rate we're going, according to the National Women's Political Caucus, we won't see political parity for more than two centuries.

It would seem, then, that we still have a long way to go. Few women in top leadership, and a pipeline barely wet with them, translates directly into unilateral male choices for how we live, and that's not good. In the words of the Reverend Patricia Kitchen, a pastor at Bryn Mawr Presbyterian Church, we need a nation of "otherism."

"For over 200 years, the United States has been steered by male leadership who tend to lead from a 'self-centered, self-preservation' perspective. (Wars declared prematurely. Inhumane tax structures adopted. Environmental disregard. Labor practices which devalue workers. Third world sweatshops that crush the souls of foreign labor . . . all seem to serve powerful 'self' interests)," she said. "Women around the world are inclined to lead, their families *and* nations, from an 'other-centered' perspective."

Despite the dangers and complexities of the world—growing armed conflicts and mounting debt, corporate irresponsibility and worldwide health crises—men don't have to give it up or go it alone. All they have to do is share power and let women help, as equals.

A World of Difference

The core of what women bring to leadership—a tendency toward greater inclusiveness, empathy, communication up and down hierarchies, focus on broader issues—makes stronger government and richer business. I saw it myself during my first decades of paid work and community service. Then it started to be named.

The first time I saw the argument in one place was 1990, when Sally Helgesen published her book *The Female Advantage.* Its broadly acclaimed central thesis: Women's skill in relationships—that ability to build webs of inclusion—was better for business than the traditional system, which concentrated power in the hands of the few.

For her research Helgesen collected information in a diary while following women executives through their workdays. Using the diary style allowed her both to identify commonalities and to compare her women to male leaders studied in the same way in 1968 by management scientist Henry Mintzberg.

Here is some of what Mintzberg found in the men he studied: an unrelenting work pace with little time for other activity, heavy identity with the job, and difficulty sharing information. Helgesen found almost the opposite in women: steady workers who also made time for on-the-job breaks and nonwork activities, who saw their jobs as only one aspect of themselves, and who scheduled time to share information in the office.

As Helgesen says, women focused on the "ecology of leadership," managing longer range. And though both genders are oriented toward the big picture, there's a difference when it comes to women: "It encompasses a vision of society—[women] relate decisions to their larger effect upon the role of the family, the American education system, the environment, even world peace."

Management guru Thomas J. Peters, coauthor of the best-selling

In Search of Excellence, agrees. He sees women as more relational, less conscious of hierarchy, better listeners, and more able to avoid the aggression men can sometimes bring to management. In fact, he published a booklet in 2001 entitled *Women Roar,* and here is how he describes it on his Web site (capitalization is his): "The evidence is clear! (1) WOMEN ARE BETTER LEADERS THAN MEN (under the conditions of the New Economy) (2) WOMEN ARE THE WORLD'S BIGGEST MARKET OPPORTUNITY (BY FAR) . . . and are wildly underserved . . . Our story: WOMEN ROAR. WOMEN RULE."

As far back as 1982, when *Excellence* was first published, Peters and his writing partner Robert H. Waterman Jr. put forward a woman-like set of management principles (though they were not identified as such at the time). More than twenty years later we have a refined Peters principle: "Women as the new economy's natural leaders." With tongue in cheek, he even suggested to an audience of radio executives in 2001 that they fire their male salespeople. "It may be against the law, but you'll be rich." He's convinced the future belongs to women: "This [women] thing is bigger than the Internet."

Before there was an Internet, before there was television—in fact, before talking movies—there was Mary Parker Follett, who may quite possibly be ground zero in the study of female-oriented management theory. I found out about her when I read a 2001 Wellesley College study on women's leadership. Follett wrote *Creative Experience* in 1924, a book that "extolled the virtues of collaboration, coordination, sharing power and information . . . empowering the workforce as opposed to having power over them." Follett saw a work world filled with interconnections. Of course, when she spoke on the topic (which was often), she would have been addressing men, since there were virtually no women leading at that time. Follett, being a woman of her own era, also didn't point out that these qualities were most often found in females; she "simply advocated the democratic, participatory style as more effective and more sound from a business perspective."

Follett's theme of collaboration has been replicated in management literature through the years. In fact, after World War II, leadership ideas very similar to hers were introduced in Japan with great enthusiasm, and they became a centerpiece of the "Japanese style." In the 1980s, this style was introduced with relish to the British and Americans; little did they know its female origins.

I remember those times well. I was director of women's programs at Drake then, helping the Des Moines business community to integrate women, whose primary experience had been in the home and community, into the workplace. The very men who impatiently asked why my "retreads" couldn't make a decision without consensus rushed to hire experts on Japanese quality circles, where workers were personally consulted about process and production. It would have been funny if it hadn't also been frustrating for the women: These men valued a so-called foreign system while devaluing the same system when it was practiced right under their noses by women.

Times have changed. Now male CEOs speak freely about their emotional intelligence, or EQ, a concept popularized in a 1995 book by Daniel Goleman that refers to components like sensitivity to others and communication skills. I heard Goleman talk about his best seller shortly after its release, and I asked him, "Aren't you largely describing women's intelligence?" He hedged, gave a nod to my point, and said half kiddingly that he wanted the book to sell. Goleman confirmed my suspicion that intelligent men knew these characteristics were very female and, therefore, very risky to embrace as such—unless you don't mind being devalued.

In the Wellesley study that resurrected Follett, sixty executive women from all walks talked about how women lead differently:

They are better communicators and listeners, more nurturing, more willing to involve others in decision making, and more likely to roll up their sleeves and work with the team. They described women as having "a much stronger sense of connectedness to others and of being part of the whole. [They] are much more gratified by leadership that involves creating a shared purpose, with the leader being part of that whole."

A root of learning for them: mothering. As a leader said, "One of the best training grounds for leadership is motherhood . . . if you can manage a group of small children, you can manage a group of bureaucrats. It's almost the same process . . ." Of those who said family was both a crucial support and a source of inspiration, all describe strong parents and grandparents: "She [grandmother] had very definite opinions about people's responsibility to contributing back to family and back to the community." One told of a father who had "an ability that you don't recognize as greatness until you're without it, which is [that] he reflected greatness in whomever he was with. He made someone else feel that they were terrific." Several of the African American women spoke of parents who cared so completely that they founded whole organizations to provide experiences their children couldn't get anywhere else, such as a swim club for a girl who couldn't use the public pool.

Elected female leadership, even the little we've had, has made a tremendous difference in politics. Prominent research groups—among them the Center for American Women and Politics at Rutgers University and the Women & Politics Institute at American University—have spent decades studying the values women bring to that arena, both in how issues are discussed and in the legislation that follows. Women, they discovered, tend to include diverse viewpoints in decision making, have a broader conception of public policy, and offer new solutions. Females also define "women's issues" more

broadly than most of their male colleagues, and they put these issues
at the top of the legislative agenda—bills dealing with children, education, and health care, for instance.

Women in politics tend to be collegial and collaborative, rather
than hierarchical. Female chairs, for example, used their leadership
positions to encourage committee members to talk with one another rather than trying to personally control and direct the debate.
We are often more responsive to constituent requests, and we follow
through on them. We are also more likely to include disadvantaged
groups in legislation. Strikingly, Republican women are more likely
than Democratic men to work on bills benefiting women. Male
politicians who were interviewed for the study agreed with the conclusions. After years of community and family involvement, women
had learned to act on the "local" model, and it worked.

Maybe all those coffee klatches finally paid off. Democratic and
Republican women of the Senate meet every month for dinner, of-
ten crossing party lines to pass legislation of importance to women.
As Senator Kay Bailey Hutchison (R–TX) reminds us, "Nobody
fought for homemakers to have retirement accounts until we [women]
did in the Senate in 1993, for God's sake." Her Senate colleague
Olympia J. Snowe (R–ME), said, "We developed the Women's Health
Equity Act . . . created an Office of Women's Health Research at the
National Institutes of Health . . . We did not allow our differing
views on abortion or our partisan affiliations to get in the way."
Other legislation critical to the health of the republic—the Family
and Medical Leave Act, the Pregnancy Discrimination Act, the
Child Support Enforcement Act—were muscled to the top by the
bipartisan Congressional Women's Caucus.

It is probably fair to say that the men in Congress, a clear majority, would not have made these issues a priority without the prod-
ding of their few female colleagues. Senator Hutchison clarifies, "It
wasn't that men were against these changes. They just hadn't consid-

ered the issue before because they hadn't experienced the problem in their own lives. As women have become a part of the system, that's changing."

Eleanor Holmes Norton, delegate to the House of Representatives from Washington, D.C., says, "Numbers matter not for numbers' sake, but for women's sake." Yes, they do, but we could also say numbers matter for *everyone's* sake. Recent research has shown a direct correlation between the number of women in a legislative body and the passage of bills benefiting women and children. However, we would need at least 15 percent of legislators to be women for a likelihood that family-friendly bills would pass. The U.S. Congress is currently 14 percent women.

Lessons from Abroad

Iceland, October 24, 1975. More than 90 percent of the women (mostly homemakers) went on strike, and the country was brought to its knees. It was described then as a "women's day off," and was originally meant as a marker for the beginning of the United Nations Decade for Women. In fact, it lives in legend as one of the most successful and swiftest social movements of all time. The strike resulted in quite a few world firsts, including the first equality legislation and the first woman president. Five years after the strike, in 1980, Vigdis Finnbogadottir was elected president, and she served until her retirement in 1996. Former President Finbogadottir likes to tell of boys who asked their mothers during her long term if men could be president of Iceland.

Women now hold at least 30 percent of the seats in the parliaments of fourteen countries, and twenty-two women are speakers of parliaments. There are seventeen women heads of state. Wales recently reached full parity between women and men in the legislature. Women in seven European countries have achieved critical mass of about a third in their parliaments: Sweden, Denmark, Finland, Norway, Iceland, the Netherlands, and Germany. A few other things these countries have in common: almost equal enrollment between boys and girls in all levels of education, comparable rates of illiteracy between both genders in the age range from fifteen to twenty-four years, and pay that is roughly equal.

The Inter-Parliamentary Union, a worldwide organization that serves as a focal point for parliamentary discussions on a broad range of issues, researched women's involvement in government and found that it brings about shifts in political behavior and priorities. Women overseas have promoted human rights issues that directly affect their lives: violence, trafficking in women, equality in marriage and parenthood, equal pay, and reproductive choice. But they don't stop there—they also raise quality-of-life issues affecting everyone, including the protection of natural resources, access to fresh water, nutrition, human rights, and protection for the destitute.

Most important, women are bringing fresh perspectives to peace building. It is not a skill new to us; it is simply not commonly acknowledged. For instance, the women of Northern Ireland have cleared the way for talks between Protestants and Catholics by bringing together key players to mediate in the strife. The women of the Sudan helped secure humanitarian aid by negotiating access directly with rebels. The women of India and Pakistan, aware of shared history amid the threat of nuclear war, have organized conventions each year to affirm their connection. As former President Bill Clinton said when the Camp David talks between the Palestinians and Israelis failed in 2000, "If we had women at Camp David, we'd have an agreement."

The United Nations is also catching on. In 2000, the Security Council issued Resolution 1325, urging the expanded role of women in field operations, "especially among military observers, civilian police, human rights workers and humanitarian personnel." Secretary-General Kofi Annan said to the council, "For generations, women have served as peace educators, both in their families and in their societies. They have proved instrumental in building bridges rather than walls."

From Theory to Action

March 3, 2003. Another powerful group of women leaders, this one global, gathered at the National Press Club in Washington, D.C. The White House Project assembled it to discuss why we matter and how to elevate more of us to power. Many U.S. heavy hitters were there: Madeleine K. Albright, former secretary of state; Judy Woodruff, veteran journalist and anchor of CNN's *Inside Politics;* Charlotte Bunch, author and executive director of the Center for Women's Global Leadership at Rutgers University; Democratic pollster Celinda Lake and Republican pollster Linda DiVall; Eleanor Smeal, president of the Feminist Majority Foundation; Pat Mitchell, who runs PBS; Swanee Hunt, director of the Women and Public Policy Program at Harvard's Kennedy School of Government and former U.S. ambassador to Austria; and Ruth B. Mandel, director of the Eagleton Institute of Politics at Rutgers. They came to do what women do: teach and learn, inspire each other, and strategize for the future.

Charlotte Bunch, who has worked tirelessly to guarantee that women's rights are treated as human rights, reminded us it was women who pushed to make rape a war crime, and it was women who made sure females served on the international war crimes tribunal.

Marjorie "Mo" Mowlam, the British parliamentarian who helped broker the Good Friday Peace Agreement for Northern Ireland, spoke of the importance of networks: "The 'boys club' still operates . . . they look after each other, but not us."

Christine Pintat, formerly of the Inter-Parliamentary Union, asked a key question: Can a nation call itself a democracy when "women are so grossly underrepresented?"

Madeleine Albright observed, "If women in government do their jobs, they will improve the lot of women and girls everywhere. They will raise issues that others overlook, pass bills that others oppose, put money into projects others ignore, and seek an end to abuses others accept."

We also heard from a founder of Parité in France, Yvette Roudy, who in 1996 brought together five political women from the left and five from the right to shock the nation with their "Manifesto of the Ten," calling for equal numbers of men and women in politics. In 1999, the "Ten" and its allies got a constitutional amendment to require parity, forcing the parties to include women on their ballots or incur a financial penalty. After the amendment passed, female representation on city councils nearly doubled, jumping from 25.5 percent to 47.5 percent. Roudy, who lived up to the pronunciation of her name (rowdy), insisted that we be more daring. She also urged young women to "seek public office, because it is in politics that you can bring about social change and improvement."

In 1989, with fifty-five years of democracy under its belt, India still had a parliament that was only 8 percent women. This was the motivation for Ranjana Kumari, director of the Centre for Social Research in India. She and others traveled broadly, collecting signatures for a constitutional amendment that would reserve a third of all village council seats for women. It passed, and 1.3 million women now serve their villages in a whole new way. Kumari is working to extend this fairness in representation to the national level.

Anita Gradin of Sweden, former member of parliament, pushed legislation that put her country nearly on top in women's political participation: 45.3 percent. She advocated "strong women's organizations to pressure, to work with the parties, to push them both from the inside and out—the men will not do it for us."

Sheila Sisulu, one of the apartheid freedom fighters who insisted on (and got) a power guarantee for women, reminded us that "we don't have to be superwomen. We don't have to do it all by ourselves. We can make alliances, including with men, to make us effective."

But the crowning moment came at the conclusion of a round table where fourteen experts in American politics, policy, organizing, and academics discussed how our country could increase women's political representation. After several questions from the floor, a woman rose majestically and introduced herself as Gwen Mahlangu, a representative in the South African parliament and president of the Inter-Parliamentary Union's Coordinating Committee of Women Parliamentarians. She marveled that America, for all its progress, was still so backward in advancing women in politics. And, with a conviction that took our breath away, she offered to help us become a democracy: "I will stand by you, sisters, I will stand by you."

▰ ▰ ▰

Since the conference, I think often of Gwen. I also think of those women in India, boarding a train every day, rumbling through heat and dust, setting up colorful tables at each whistle-stop to attract attention and to provide a gathering place, telling poor and illiterate women that they matter, changing lives one signature at a time. And I hear the question of France's Yvette Roudy: "Since women matter, why are they not in places where important decisions are taken? Why are they not in national and international assemblies, in financial boards, in other places of power?"

Good question. It is time for an answer, and it lies within the barriers we erect to women's leadership.

2

BARRIERS TO LEADERSHIP

Many traits traditionally valued of women also
perpetuate women's inequality.

—*Deborah L. Rhode, professor
and expert on gender equality,
Stanford University Law School*

Eighty-seven percent of Americans are willing to vote for a qualified woman for president.

Seventy-six percent of "influential Americans" think she'll be elected within twenty years.

If the 2004 election was held today, and if a woman were on the Democratic ticket as vice president, six separate subgroups of women (and one subgroup of men) would cross party lines to vote for her.

These statistics come from three different polls, all done in 2003, all indicating a desire for women's leadership at the pinnacle of government. Why, then, if we say we're almost ready to elect a woman president, haven't we closed the gap throughout politics, and in business? Why do the paltry numbers of women at the top belie the opposite sentiment for putting them there?

The answer is buried in a host of barriers—cultural and emotional, societal and historical—that keep women from gaining traction. We must also deal with perceptions—both of what a leader looks like (sometimes literally) and that women already run the world, even though the statistics say otherwise. In fact, one of our major problems is that we think we have no problem.

It is what Betty Friedan, in her 1963 classic *The Feminine Mystique,* called "the problem that has no name," and what Deborah L. Rhode, law professor at Stanford University and expert on gender equality, calls "the 'no problem' problem." Most Americans don't realize how far we *haven't* come. We like to think we live in a fair country with a level playing field, that hard work and talent will prevail, that discrimination against women happened long, long ago on somebody else's watch. We remain in denial despite evidence such as the sea of men on the floor of Congress or in newspaper business sections any day of the week.

Americans tend to ignore the societal and cultural foot dragging at the root of the matter, often failing to recognize deeply embedded gender roles that, for all our advancement, have kept our nation from realizing its potential. As the essayist Katha Pollitt says, "Americans have a curiously shallow understanding of the relationship of the individual to society: we greatly underestimate the role of social forces in making us what we are and in limiting our real, as opposed to abstract, choices."

And we rarely admit that we limit choices through gender alone. The White House Project watched this principle in action during the 2002 gubernatorial elections. Twenty-six women filed to run for governor in twenty states, and ten of them won their primaries. Strong candidates—among them state attorneys general and treasurers—seemed poised for victory, bringing female experience and visibility to a job that is considered a feeder to the presidency. In spite of their résumés, however, we knew these candidates would be judged by impossible standards—tough and caring, Joan of Arc and Mother Teresa. We thought we'd try to help.

Since elections can be won and lost through media, we studied past TV ads of both genders. Were there templates from old campaigns, examples of women who projected themselves as leaders with a heart, and still won? And how do those templates differ for men? We reviewed nearly four hundred spots throughout recent political history, starting in the 1990s. What a kick they were to watch: Ann Richards of Texas, Madeleine M. Kunin of Vermont, Christine Todd Whitman of New Jersey. We picked the cream of the ads, mostly from unknown candidates, and got to work.

A diverse "audience" of voters was handpicked to view the ads and react to them through a dial they turned up or down to measure the traits that made candidates effective. But that was not the only lesson we learned; we also discovered "face credibility." Before the ads even started, when the candidates simply appeared on the screen without speaking a word—in fact, before he or she had any real traits at all other than gender—the dialers made decisions about leadership potential. Women stayed even or were dialed down, but men were dialed up from the first second. Women had to dig out, to prove they were worthy of the attention and the elected office before their scores turned positive. Men had the instant advantage, based on their maleness.

The very word "leadership" conjures images for most of us. It can evoke a historical figure like Mahatma Gandhi or someone in our own lives—perhaps a coach or a teacher—who made a difference. Unfortunately, it does not automatically bring to mind many women. We ran focus groups after the gubernatorial session with the dials, and I vividly recall a man wanting to know for *certain* if one of the women had been a leader, yet he did not ask the same of any man.

Shirley Franklin, the first female mayor of Atlanta and the first black woman to lead a large southern city, had spent a decade at the heart of the city's day-to-day operations. In the 1970s she worked for Mayor Maynard Jackson, and she virtually ran the place in the 1980s when she was chief administrative officer for Mayor Andrew J. Young. Yet, as she told an audience in 2002 at Emory University, during her campaign many people were shocked that she knew so much about the inner workings of government.

After receiving the dial test results, we convened a group of New York businesswomen to share the findings, thinking they would be interested in the barriers we found for women politicians. Far beyond interest, these executives informed us that they *were* this study, since they faced the same perception problems as the female candidates. In fact, a poll from July 2003 on MBACareers.com backs them up, showing that men and women get advanced business degrees for very different reasons: men to prepare for entrepreneurship and advancement, women to increase their career opportunities and for *credibility.* Men did not list credibility as a motivator.

How, then, do we counter this problem of being seen as "less than" by virtue of genetics? How do we dislodge barriers that, unlike the blatant discrimination of old, can be more subtle yet still keep women from leadership? It cannot be a one-step process because the problems are everywhere: in the television shows we watch, in the newspapers we read, in the advertising we scan, in the psyches we develop as we navigate societal expectations of us as men and women. The only way to stop it is to change the rules, inside and out, individually and collectively, rewriting the definition of "leader" and putting a woman's face on it.

Tough as Nails, Warm as Toast

"Just be patient. It's only a matter of time."

That's true when it comes to women at the top, but your willingness to accept this platitude as an answer to the leadership gap depends on your definition of "time." As we have seen, parity can take several centuries. Most of us are in a bigger hurry than that.

The pipeline theory of women's ascendancy is definitely the means to an end: Insert enough women at all levels and their promotion to higher business ranks or election to higher office is statistically inevitable. And critical mass, when it is achieved, will raise the comfort level of the women in that pipeline and women already at the top. But the flow through the pipeline is currently only a trickle (even though it is perceived to be otherwise), and it is limiting the number of women who reach the upper echelons.

If, for instance, the pipeline to the presidency is Congress, 86 percent are men; if it is governorships, 88 percent are men. Half of our top elected leaders first ran for office before they were thirty-five years old; of young politicians today, who would be a pipeline to Congress and governorships, 86 percent are men. If the pipeline to top leadership in business is "line positions" (those with revenue-generating or profit-and-loss responsibility), 90.1 percent are men. Men also hold 92.1 percent of "clout" titles (those that wield the most policy-making power).

So the "female advantage" is still not taking hold, either at the top or in feeder positions to it. Why? Because this style of leadership and the traits that accompany it, such as inclusiveness, broader focus on issues, communication, and empathy—all typically associated with women, and central to family and community systems—have never found value in the corporate or political worlds in America. Male assertiveness and control continue to be in higher demand.

What's interesting is that powerful men with an inner female (as long as it's pulled out for display purposes only) are canonized. Former mayor Rudolph W. Giuliani of New York City, a classic ball-buster, became a national hero because of the way he handled September 11, most of which had to do with showing a softer side.

President George W. Bush, when running in 2000, knew he had to appeal to women if he wanted to win, so his handlers latched onto "compassionate conservatism" (which, according to the *New York Times,* could become a liability in his reelection campaign because he has fallen far short of his goals for education and AIDS).

We often find resistance to women's leadership because they are not seen as tough enough, both due to the male-oriented definition of "leader" and the entrenched "cultural ideal" of female: sensitive and warm, self-sacrificing and nurturing, good wife and mother. These assets, while valued in the home, become reasons to marginalize women on the job.

There is much talk in the modern office of the virtues of a democratic "female" form of leadership, but it is more rhetoric than reality, especially when you get near the top. Nurturing male leaders will almost never be seen as dynamic, and if you attach typical male toughness to a woman, she becomes a bitch. Neither gender can act out of the box without consequences.

It is a juggling act even the Cirque du Soleil couldn't pull off: Women can try to prove they're "man enough," but they'll never be accepted for it; yet if they bring their whole female selves into the workplace, they're devalued. As Professor Rhode of Stanford put it, "Most Americans believe that women should exhibit [traits like sensitivity, warmth, self-sacrifice, nurturance, and physical attractiveness], and a majority of women view 'being feminine' as central to how they define themselves. Yet few individuals realize how often these expectations restrict women's opportunities for self-fulfillment . . ." In the words of author and columnist Anna Quindlen, we've got to be "tough as nails and warm as toast."

Redefining "Leader"

So once we get to the workplace, we already have two strikes against us: one, that we *are* females, which doesn't match the physical look of a leader, and two, that the qualities we bring do not match the traditional actions of a leader. Add to that the structural impediments to anyone (male or female) who might like to be a parent *and* a worker—no child care, little flexibility in work hours—and you've made it nearly impossible for a woman to work, let alone rise. (Men, at least, can usually count on wives to pick up the slack.)

Careerwomen.com, in a 2003 poll on women and career advancement, pointed to barriers in the corporate culture, among them exclusion from informal networks, a culture that clearly favors men, the small number of women serving in senior management (which, if fixed, might solve the other two), and a continuing perception that family will get in the way. The Web site quoted one respondent: "Work/life balance is difficult for women. Children, aging parents, home responsibilities all seem to be women's issues." Another said, "When seeking a promotion, I always considered that I can do it all—I don't think this is a consideration of my male colleagues."

Often the accepted way of getting ahead at work correlates to the number of hours you put in. Women can't win there either, even if they want to do the time. A 2001 RoperASW poll found that most Americans find it more acceptable for men to work overtime (56 percent), even if it means being away from their families. On the other hand, it is more acceptable for women to give up a career to stay at home and care for the family (73 percent). And what of men who don't want to work as hard as they often feel they must, who want to spend more time with their wife and kids? They can, but they risk their careers—some find themselves "warned" about the consequences and, if they do it anyway, derailed from the fast track, just like women.

Society expects, and even demands, that females absorb the "second shift" of home and family, even if they work somewhere else too. If government and industry really valued women at work, they would make it easier for them to be there, creating programs and flexibility in the job itself. There is a perception that most companies provide enormous options for working parents, but it's not true.

A 2002 study by the Families and Work Institute found employees experiencing much higher levels of "interference" between work and family life than those surveyed in 1977. Flexibility in hours has been introduced by some employers, but there has been no change since the early 1990s in employer-sponsored and/or -operated child care (10 percent), which puts a real burden on parents (especially women).

Part of the reason: the expense. As the essayist Katha Pollitt points out, "To equalize the standings of men and women would cost billions of dollars, require the overhaul of many institutions and destabilize many kinds of personal and professional relationships." Technology has made it more possible, and cheaper, with devices like cell phones and Blackberrys that provide instant and constant connectivity. But there's an unacknowledged sociological fact that goes beyond e-mail: High-ranking jobs, and the ability to do them well, are based on a two-person model—one on the front lines of work and one in support of that effort at home. Furthermore, that model is based on an old gender dictate, still in place: Society feels more comfortable with men on the front lines and women in the house. The modern-day twist on the ancient imperative is that women can also work, as long as they keep the domestic trains running on time. Both genders are locked into an expectation of what they will do to support the American way of life.

We need a new definition of "leader"—one that looks and

sounds like a woman too—and we've got to set up the structures (institutional and societal) that will allow this newly defined leader to really go to work. We need child care and other parent-friendly programs, and we need to end, once and for all, women's deal with society to be the sole caregivers.

As we all know, it has gone on for centuries, this "agreement" that we derive power from the private realm, leaving the public sphere to men. This deal was institutionalized by the church fathers of the sixteenth century, when the twin mantles of "True Womanhood" and holiness became linked to our roles as mothers. Women would shape the democracy by raising children; men would control industry and government. Women would be kept far from the nasty business of running the world, ensuring our purity and ethics would be passed to subsequent generations. Men would make whatever bargains were required to protect and provide for their families.

This unratified pact sailed from Europe, found salience in the newly formed republic, and was documented extensively by Alexis de Tocqueville when he visited the United States in the nineteenth century. Though he found women "confined within the narrow circle of domestic life" in a situation of "extreme dependence," he also felt that if he were asked "to what the singular prosperity and growing strength of that people ought mainly to be attributed, I should reply: To the superiority of their women."

Two centuries later, even after women have entered the workforce in record numbers (mostly in jobs earning an average of $32,641 a year, compared to the male average of $50,557), the "cultural ideal" of wife and mother has changed little. Women are still expected, and expect themselves, to serve the family above all else, ensuring the burden of two full-time jobs, since most have to work outside the home to help support families. Men are still given a pass to put most of their energy into the office, often at the expense of the family.

The historical bargain of public versus private has come at a very high cost, and both genders have paid the price. Men's families often grow up without them. Women remain underappreciated for their home and community labors; and if they have jobs, they rarely rise to executive levels. Because we occupy so few positions of ultimate authority, our diverse and divergent viewpoints are not inserted into vital discussions. Men are still left to be men, without much opportunity to act differently as workers, fathers, and husbands, even when they want to. Women remain unheard. The democracy continues to function without critical input that would shape it into a fairer system with fresh ideas.

It's exciting to imagine what a nation of women working for the common good could do, especially when you consider the monumental work of one woman in a more rigid time: Eleanor Roosevelt. ER was an unintentional deal breaker, a woman orphaned and mostly unloved whose schooling in social justice began when she was shipped off to study in England during adolescence. She married her cousin Franklin and quickly assumed the traditional role, allowing him the slack to rise to prominence as she managed their complex and child-filled private life.

Ultimately her compensation for spousal support was betrayal when Franklin had an affair with his personal secretary. Eleanor was crushed and immobile for almost a year before she turned her grief into a new deal for herself. Her life of strictly private power was over and she determined to use her public voice as a public person speaking on public policies. In both Franklin's New York gubernatorial race in 1928 and his presidential run in 1931, she got out the women's vote and pushed women's concerns to the front burner of the campaigns. Along with the chair of women's activities for the Democratic Party, she drew up a list of potential candidates and worked hard to secure their appointments—by 1935, over sixty women were in national positions and hundreds more in state and local government agencies.

Through her constant intervention, ER brought the concerns of the disenfranchised to the attention of the press and the president. The result: a new deal for herself and a New Deal for Americans struggling in the depth of the Depression that is a hallmark of compassionate human welfare and economic development. This revolutionary legislation, hailed as "a masterpiece of Presidential leadership," owed much of its existence to the first lady, who may not have had ultimate authority, but who by then was president of her own life.

The Popular Culture

Eleanor Roosevelt's many means to an end included the culture. She wrote extensively and she was a fixture on the radio—two media where Americans came to know her and to love her. Her sponsored radio program gave listeners a women's perspective, and starting in 1936, United Features carried her syndicated column six days a week. ER understood the opportunity, and she used it well.

The popular culture—television, movies, journalism, advertising, and books—presents enormous opportunity for crafting a new vision of women in society. It has the power to redefine "leader," to normalize the sight and sound of a woman in charge at the highest levels.

Whether we like it or not, we are deeply, subliminally affected by media-defined leaders, and women have a long way to go to be among them. Channel surf and you'll see two men (one of them African American, thank goodness) playing U.S. presidents in prime-time dramas. Every A-list male actor in Hollywood has had a shot at a silver screen presidency. Click to the Sunday morning talk shows and you'll see that men outnumber women nine to one in guest appearances. We may see more women on stage and screen, but there is a difference between leading lady and leader, and between occasional talk show guest and regular pundit. It is critical to remember that the way in which a woman appears, in fact and fiction, will often determine her status and authority, just as it does for men.

A good example in real life is the stage-managing of President George W. Bush. In May 2003, he made a well-publicized landing on the aircraft carrier *Abraham Lincoln,* leaping onto the deck in a "top gun" flight suit and giving a speech to T-shirted, color-coordinated sailors. In the background, at the perfect angle for cameras, a massive sign said: MISSION ACCOMPLISHED. We now know how much hyperbole lay behind that message, and how little the president knew about flying. But the country was left with the image of a manly man at the controls. I could call it reality TV, but it's much too scripted for that. It's pure Hollywood. (Now, of course, as the Iraqi situation deteriorates, that sign's message is backfiring on him. At a press conference in October 2003, President Bush said the idea came from the sailors themselves, but "no one seems to want to take credit" for it.)

The real Hollywood gives us women, many women, but mostly as support staff to male stars, though it was still marvelous to see Glenn Close play the vice president in *Air Force One.* Another recent example who breaks the pattern is Julia Roberts (among the few women who can carry a picture) in the title role as the whistleblower Erin Brockovich. There's also Reese Witherspoon, different from the recent heroines for her feminine moxie, in both *Legally Blonde* movies. Longer ago, we had Sally Field's *Norma Rae* and Meryl Streep's *Silkwood.* Today's woman-as-leader in film and television tends to be an action figure, a turbo version of the Bond girls of the James Bond classics—for instance, Angelina Jolie in *Tomb Raider,* an Indiana Jones knockoff, and Jennifer Garner in ABC's *Alias.*

The heroine of *Tomb Raider,* Lara Croft, is powerful and soft, sexy and principled. Or at least that's Lara Croft the movie figure. Then there's Lara Croft the action figure in video games. In the original version, her chest was expansively unreal; women complained. In the upgrade it will be smaller—and you'll be happy to know she won't simply shoot and run; she'll fight the bad guys hand to hand. In fact, she's a pinup for men and boys, who constitute the vast majority of video game players.

Is this progress? Is this leadership? Doubtful. For one thing, it sends the unreal message that women are strong in life—literally as strong as men—and they most certainly are not. The characters are hyperwomen with stylized bodies, yet they act like the stereotypical male warrior. As feminist theorist bell hooks points out, the message here is to join patriarchy, not challenge it. "They take people's minds away from really how much power females are losing in real life," she said. They create a perception that women are strong and in charge, which most aren't, and they don't lead our imagination to real power: the presidency or CEO of a corporation. If we really want to change perceptions, we'll demand that media and culture portray us beating the *intellectual* daylights out of our opponents.

Our Scarlet A's

I recently reread Nathaniel Hawthorne's nineteenth-century novel of seventeenth-century morality, *The Scarlet Letter.* In the book a woman is forced to wear a scarlet A to signify her break with society through her adultery. It got me to thinking of the real scarlet A's in our lives, the ways we are minimized and defined, ways we are kept in our place, and ways we keep ourselves from the life we might lead. The A's that resound for me: authority, ambition, ability, and authenticity.

Throughout history we have largely been denied the authority to command on a grand scale since so few of us have reached the top in any sector. Ambition, a hallmark of manhood, is considered to be unwomanly, and sometimes downright unnatural. (In support of the argument, I offer three words: Hillary Rodham Clinton, who was virtually tortured for wanting to be a "working" first lady.) Despite our natural and learned abilities, we tend to be trusted less often than less qualified men. And in the process of negotiating authority, ambition, and ability, we can sometimes lose the core of who we are— our authenticity, our genuine voice, our willingness to see the world differently and insist upon changing it.

Transforming these barriers to women's leadership into opportunities seems an impossibly grand ambition. As it stands, we have a definition of "leader" that leaves little room for women and the qualities we bring, an unwelcoming workplace that makes it tough for either gender (but especially women) to have a balanced life, a culture that steadfastly refuses to show women in leadership roles, and the A's, those words whose current meanings sabotage women from all angles. Before we throw up our hands and get back to the laundry, we should remember that women with tougher lives than ours managed to stand up and be counted.

Take Abigail Adams, wife of one president (John) and mother of another (John Quincy). Read excerpts of the correspondence between husband and wife during the American Revolution in 1776:

Abigail to John:

> I long to hear that you have declared an independency. And, by the way, in the new code of laws, which I suppose it will be necessary for you to make, I desire you would remember the ladies and be more generous and favorable to them than your ancestors. Do not put such unlimited power into the hands of the husbands. Re-

member, all men would be tyrants if they could. If particular care and attention is not paid to the ladies, we are determined to foment a rebellion, and will not hold ourselves bound by any laws in which we have no voice or representation . . .

John to Abigail (obviously, he didn't take her seriously):

As to your extraordinary code of laws, I cannot but laugh. We have been told that our struggle has loosened the bounds of government everywhere; that children and apprentices were disobedient; that schools and colleges were grown turbulent; that Indians slighted their guardians, and Negroes grew insolent to their masters. But your letter was the first intimation that another tribe, more numerous and powerful than all the rest, were grown discontented. This is rather too coarse a compliment, but you are so saucy, I won't blot it out. Depend upon it, we know better than to repeal our masculine systems. Although they are in full force, you know they are little more than theory. We dare not exert our power in its full latitude. We are obliged to go fair and softly, and, in practice, you know we are the subjects. We have only the name of masters, and rather than give this up, which would completely subject us to the despotism of the petticoat, I hope General Washington and all our brave heroes would fight.

Abigail to John (thoroughly annoyed):

I cannot say I think you are very generous to the ladies; for, whilst you are proclaiming peace and goodwill toward men, emancipating all nations, you insist upon retaining an absolute power over wives. But you must remember that arbitrary power is like most other things which are very hard, very liable to be broken; and, notwithstanding all your wise laws and maxims, we have it in our power, not only to free ourselves, but to subdue our masters, and without violence, throw both your natural and legal authority at our feet.

Abigail couldn't make good on her threat to John, and he knew it. For one thing, she didn't have other women as support; for another, "leader" equaled "man" at that time, hands down; and finally, she was firmly stuck in the social fabric of her day, though not so much that she didn't feel empowered to say her piece. Nor should we, especially since we have the privilege of a different world.

So many feisty potential presidents have passed our way: Sojourner Truth, Susan B. Anthony, Shirley Chisholm, Barbara Jordan, Eleanor Roosevelt, and for my money, Abigail Adams. Even now, beyond the women currently serving in high office, there are thousands of local women, names unfamiliar, ready to serve, filled with resources of courage and vision, eager to transform their communities and their country. Perhaps they will even transform the world. They're "nobody" now, without financial or political capital. We desperately need them to raise their hands and offer to serve, to endure the inevitable slings and arrows until they're no longer alone, to show future generations what it truly means to lead.

3

AUTHORITY

It is important for women to not just be in office, but in power. Women must be in power
before we can be said to be equal.

—Marjorie "Mo" Mowlam,
member of British Parliament

If we intend to dismantle the barriers to women's leadership, one of
the first we should tackle is authority. Women must be seen as com-
manding and powerful, as the place where the buck stops, in the
words of Harry Truman's famous Oval Office plaque. It's not so easy,
especially when our society upholds "the masculinity of authority
and the authority of masculinity."

I know this struggle well.

In Iowa in the early eighties, I was one of a handful of people
who knew something about job sharing. I had built one of the
largest divisions of women's programming in the country at Drake
University, and within it were some of the earliest experiments in alternative work arrangements. I constantly fielded calls from top university and government officers, all wanting to know how we had
accomplished so much.

During that time, two teachers in the Des Moines school system sought a job share, a rarity in those days. The school district didn't want to go to that unfamiliar, possibly costly place—now more accepted in America—so the teachers sued. I was called to testify on their behalf.

The attorney for the school district addressed the judge while I was on the stand with words that shocked me: "Your Honor, this witness is no expert." No expert? How could he say that? The worst part was—and I cringe to remember it—I almost believed this relative stranger, who labeled himself an expert on *me*.

Like millions of women, then and now, I had acquired positional authority, but it went unrecognized. The power and influence that should have accrued from my knowledge and experience had eluded me beyond my narrow circle, as it had (and has) for most women, no matter how learned or successful. I *was* an expert, I *was* an authority, but the perception was otherwise because I didn't match the definition or the look.

There are thousands of examples like mine, and it is the very ordinariness of them that makes them so profound. How many women have contributed their best at meetings only to find that when a man says the same thing moments later, it is hailed as genius—and his idea. I laughed recently with author Sally Helgesen as we compared prespeech introductions that were so limp we spent the first twenty minutes rebuilding a solid platform of authority with the audience. I would always prefer to be described by someone like Sally Minard, head of the Women's Leadership Forum and former owner of a public relations firm in New York City. Even in private introductions, Sally makes you want to know *yourself* better.

According to a 2003 newspaper article in England, five female parliamentarians went the artificial route to bolster their authority. A doctor reportedly gave them testosterone implants to boost "their assertiveness and [make] them feel more powerful." I hope by now they know that their bodies were not the barriers that needed transforming.

Sometimes, though, you're damned no matter what you do. "It doesn't matter what I say about an issue. If I have a run in my panty hose, that's all anybody will talk about," said Senator Blanche Lincoln (D-AR). In 1984, when Geraldine Ferraro was running for vice president, Woodrow Paige, columnist for the *Denver Post,* offered this about her history-making campaign: "Ferraro has nicer legs than any previous vice presidential candidate." The next woman to run for high office from a major party did not fare much better, despite the passage of time.

The Candidacy of Elizabeth Dole

In 1999, Elizabeth Hanford Dole (now *Senator* Dole, after being elected in 2000 to represent North Carolina) was running for the highest office in the land with a stunning résumé: former cabinet secretary in two administrations and former president of the American Red Cross. If anyone deserved a mantle of authority, she did. Most media coverage, however, concentrated on her well-known prickly side and her uncomfortable relationship with the press. From the *New York Times:* "Dole prepares so thoroughly for appearances that she even requires aides to count the steps she must take to the podium. Though roughly as fragile as Margaret Thatcher, she is also famously thin-skinned, and has been known to burst into tears over unflattering press."

That quote is the tip of the iceberg. Both Rutgers University and the White House Project did comprehensive studies in 2000 of Dole's six-month candidacy, which ended before the first primary and offers a unique window into the press coverage of a female presidential candidate. Among the conclusions: Dole was covered more as a novelty than a serious candidate. "Despite being the second most popular Republican candidate in public opinion polls and a likely winner if matched against [Democratic Vice President] Al Gore . . . Dole was mentioned in only one out of every five articles." She was covered along gender lines "in ways that likely hindered her candidacy."

In the preprimary months of Dole's run, Senator John McCain (R-AZ), just another face in the crowd then, received twice as many mentions in press articles. The media coverage of Dole was not only less frequent, it was also less substantial—inconsistent with her standing as number two in the polls and guaranteed to tamp down her authority. Compared to other candidates, Dole's personal appearance was mentioned far more often, and some mentions were extremely negative. The *Detroit News:* Her "public speaking style looks and sounds like Tammy Faye Baker meets the Home Shopping Network." The *Los Angeles Times:* "Fabric . . . will shine, crinkle, stretch, seem like paper, have a sheer veneer or be tougher than, say, Elizabeth Dole's hairdo." The study points out that no such "degrading references" were found for any of the men against whom she ran.

It's tough to be one of a kind, especially when it becomes the main identifier of who you are, as it did for Dole in article after article. Another focus—her lack of a campaign war chest—might have negatively influenced the public by planting the seed that she was not a viable candidate; success in politics is intimately linked to fundraising.

All the way to the end she remained number two behind George W. Bush, a man with far fewer credentials. And yet another man, John McCain, rocketed to prominence ahead of her, quite possibly because of his plethora of positive press. "The unusual level and positive nature of McCain's coverage helped him go from a relatively unknown candidate to almost stealing the nomination" from Bush.

Even Dole's husband, former Senate leader and 1996 presidential candidate Bob Dole, suggested he might make a contribution to McCain (can you imagine what would happen if a woman did that to her husband?).

Would Elizabeth Dole have won if her press coverage hadn't been gender biased? Who can say? But the case of John McCain (and, more recently, former Vermont governor Howard Dean and general Wesley Clark) clearly shows that when the press confers authority, it can nearly take an unknown candidate to the White House.

Hair, Hemlines, and Husbands

Any focus on the superficial will always erode authority; the phrase "just another pretty face" is not for nothing. In fact, in 1998 we were so struck by press obsession with the personal aspects of women that the White House Project chose it as our first media study. We looked at the coverage of general election campaigns of women running for governor in Arizona, Colorado, Maryland, and Rhode Island that year, as well as two hotly contested Democratic primaries in Massachusetts, one for governor and one for attorney general. The results came to be called our "hair, hemlines, and husbands" research. We weren't surprised to find that women were covered less substantively and more personally than men, but we were taken aback by the pervasiveness of it.

We analyzed press clips from these six campaigns (311 newspaper stories totaling 3,326 paragraphs and 891 candidate quotes), and here's some of what we found:

- Journalists were more likely to focus on the personal characteristics of female candidates, with differences in coverage based on the gender of

the reporter. While women journalists reported
on personal aspects for both women and men,
male journalists more frequently covered the age
and marital and family status (most notably the
presence or absence of offspring) of female candidates.

- Reporters were more likely to highlight male
candidates' positions and records on the issues
and were more likely to quote male candidates'
reasoning behind their claims.

A woman who speaks with authority can find herself buried by
it. After we released our research at the National Press Club, I made
a point to talk to the Democratic candidate for governor of Rhode
Island, Myrth York. When it came to stories with backup, our data
showed the gap between her and her male opponent was larger than
any other candidate. Why? Throughout the campaign, reporters
continually complained to York that she was *too* substantive.

This coverage of women—more personal, less issue based, and
less likely to include evidence to support their quoted remarks—
undermines authority, leaving the impression that women don't understand and cannot handle real power. It makes working and winning
that much harder, decreasing the size of the pipeline to leadership by
a sin of omission and convincing Americans that men are the real
experts.

Gail Schoettler is another case study. She was the lieutenant governor of Colorado, running for governor in 1999, and her résumé
included the following: founder, board member, and board chair of
two banks; cochair of the successful 1997 Summit of the Eight
world leaders in Denver; two-term treasurer for the State of Colorado; doctorate in history from the University of California. Dr.
Schoettler was thought to have an excellent chance of winning, but

read this description in the *Rocky Mountain News:* "Schoettler shows up at glitzy campaign to-dos in a dusty 1993 Toyota with cans of apricot nectar and granola bars sliding around on the floorboards." This characterization as an eccentric, unkempt woman helped to undo years of competence and experience. Dr. Schoettler lost to her Republican opponent.

Who's Talking

Women are rarely seen and almost never positioned as leaders by the press, whose coverage of them is usually light in content and volume. Most of the time authorities are picked from a small, elite male pool: members of Congress, titans of industry, presidential candidates, and other journalists. This very narrow band relegates the rest of us (including most women) to watchers rather than doers. When we do get our day in the headlines, our authority tends to be challenged more often, our statements scrutinized more thoroughly than those of men.

"Our male counterparts can say whatever they want," said Representative Rosa DeLauro (D-CT). "It can make sense or not make sense. But women have to work much harder . . . For women, there is always that little bit of built-in insecurity about having to know every single thing about every single thing when you stand up."

Mellody Hobson, president of a successful Chicago-based minority-owned financial firm, Ariel Capital Management, says she is sometimes discounted for the trifecta of race, gender, and youth. To counter it, she feels she must "establish my authority by being an expert, and by always, always, always being prepared." This can mean staying up all night to ready a presentation. She also reads five newspapers a day because she assumes that others size her up by what she knows.

I saw the same phenomenon in the 1970s when I was a management trainer helping to integrate men and women as colleagues into the workplace. Through exercises we would explore a wide range of company policies. Men always spoke authoritatively about these policies, but later, when the women asked the men how they knew so much verbatim, the men admitted they had been winging it with their answers; the women never did that, and only spoke when they had all the facts. As explanation, the men simply said they knew they could correct their responses later if need be. The women felt they would never get a second chance if they misspoke.

Nowhere is public anointment more critical—and more absolute—than in the media. When almost no women are put forward as "experts," it creates an impression that there are precious few competent females. *All* women are then painted with the brush of mediocrity, though their real problem is simply that they are not being selected to give their views. They are not selected because they do not fit the narrow criteria the media use to define "expert." Authority continues to be concentrated in the hands of men and, as a consequence, women remain outside the power elite.

Our invisibility is never so obvious than on the five most important Sunday talk shows. The White House Project analyzed these network shows for eighteen months, from January 1, 2000, to June 30, 2001. The results, published in a survey called *Who's Talking,* confirmed our armchair suspicions: Men outnumbered women nine to one in guest appearances on *This Week* (ABC), *Face the Nation* (CBS), *Late Edition with Wolf Blitzer* (CNN), *Fox News Sunday* (FOX), and *Meet the Press* (NBC).

Sunday morning talk shows have enormous influence in shaping the next week's issues and in creating awareness of policy. These shows have what media scholars call an agenda-setting effect; as a result, they confer expert status on the guests they choose, raising their profile through exposure on our nation's most popular medium. They also have an authority-setting effect: They tell us who can be trusted to deal with complex global issues. When women are rarely shown in the hot seat, two things occur: First, women fail to be seen as authorities by the millions of viewers tuning in each weekend. Second, only the opinions of men are heard, thereby losing a female perspective. It affects not only the way the country views women, but also the manner in which problems are solved, limiting the range of solutions by limiting the variety of opinions.

When we showed the study to producers, one of them told us, "If the women were there, we'd put them on." ("There" means in positions of authority.) We pointed out the number of times this producer had invited Senator John Edwards of North Carolina, first-term senator and at that time a relative newcomer, to appear on the air. She replied that he was a potential Democratic candidate for vice president. We showed her how many times he had been on *before* he was a potential candidate. The producer was taken aback that Edwards's Sunday morning exposure might have *made* him politically viable.

The most troubling aspect of the study was that these shows often sought out-of-power men rather than the women who were currently in charge. During the eighteen months of our study, the male *former* heads of the Republican and Democratic Senate Campaign Committees were on the shows twenty-four times and sixteen times, respectively, but the chair of the Democratic Senatorial Campaign Committee at that time—Senator Patty Murray (D-WA)— was not on at all.

Here's the punch line of the *Who's Talking* study: In spite of the airtight data—we did nothing more than list and count the guests on every show on every Sunday for eighteen months—the producers questioned *our* authority. They see their talking-head choices as limited by the few women in top jobs, but they overlook their ability to create new female leaders, as they have done with men, and to enlist fresh outlooks with refreshing solutions.

We added a month to our study of the talk shows after the shocking events of September 11, 2001, to see if women would be put forward as leaders. They weren't. In fact, the number of women dropped from nine to one before the terrorist attacks to thirteen to one afterward. We were flabbergasted, especially since the Senate's three principal subcommittees on terrorism were all chaired by women. None were on the talk shows after September 11. Senator Kay Bailey Hutchison (R-TX), the ranking member on the Commerce Committee's Subcommittee on Aviation, was also not a guest, nor was Representative Nancy Pelosi of California, the ranking Democrat on the House Intelligence Committee. It almost seemed intentional.

A review of the same shows from February 2 to April 27, 2003 (as the war in Iraq began), which included full transcripts from NBC's *Meet the Press* and CNN's *Late Edition* and partial transcripts from the other three Sunday shows, wasn't reassuring. They continue to skew heavily toward male guests. On *Meet the Press,* arguably the nation's most watched and most quoted Sunday program, only 8.8 percent (or four out of forty-five) of the guests were female. Not one woman met the press on nine different Sundays, and on three of the weekends there was only one female guest on all the networks combined.

In Washington, D.C., when we presented the data from our original talk show study, many women in Congress showed up to bear witness. Representative Marcy Kaptur (D-OH) spoke powerfully about the recent past on the floor of Congress, where women spoke and men never paused to listen, their voices creating a dull roar that filled the chamber.

Congresswoman Kaptur also provides a good example of un-conferred authority. She has been in office for more than two decades with a packed résumé: senior Democratic woman on the House Appropriations Committee; member of the subcommittees on agriculture, housing and urban development, environmental protection, veterans, NASA, and the National Science Foundation; honorary doctor of laws and a master's degree in urban planning. In March 2001, Kaptur announced her intention to make a major address on farm policy in Iowa, possibly laying the groundwork for a presidential run in 2004. Having been on the agriculture subcommittee, you would think she would get the benefit of the authoritative doubt on this issue. Instead: "Kaptur can't really be serious about this, can she?" said *Roll Call,* Washington's premier political magazine. How dare she think she had the gravitas to lead the country?

When our expertise is ignored, even unintentionally, our authority remains cloaked. Loosening the media barrier becomes absolutely essential to changing perceptions, to letting Americans know that knowledge and solutions are available from more than the usual suspects. It seems impossibly hard, this notion of changing the media—like turning a steamship on a dime. But it's not *that* hard, especially when we think back to times when resistance was nearly absolute.

Pushing the Power Envelope

It's been an uphill battle since the Garden of Eden. The Mother of Us All got the whole tribe kicked out of paradise (the man bears no responsibility for biting that apple, of course), leading to women's status as morally inferior, "representing emotion over reason, body over soul, and carnality over spirit. The curse as interpreted brought down on Eve's head in Eden for causing the fall of man was a punishment to be borne by generations of women living in 'sorrow and travail,'" says Constance H. Buchanan in *Choosing to Lead*.

Religion, despite its intensely private aspects, is truly a "public force," cutting the paths of both genders and determining our separate roads to authority: the World for men, the Womb for women. Those brave female souls who wanted to go public in earlier centuries had to improvise in a big way, turning religion and family on their heads to gain broader status. The early abolitionists and female social reformers are perfect examples, since they used the very religious belief system that limited them as reason to take on social change outside the home, to do God's work of "perfecting the world."

Early suffragists in the twentieth century knew there could be no authority without the vote, and they managed their arguments strictly by tradition. They used the stereotypes of women as virtuous wives and mothers to justify this right: Wouldn't all society benefit by having citizens of our caliber casting a ballot? They used women's role as the caretakers of children—a place where we still have undiminished authority—as a reason for enfranchisement: Wouldn't females be more likely to support public positions on the eradication of child labor? Reformer Jane Addams of the early twentieth century even equated politics to "large-scale housekeeping."

The scope of authority expanded over time, as did the issues women tackled. The powerful temperance movement found its leadership in outraged mothers seeking an end to the violence of drunks in the nineteenth century, thus protecting the entire community. Improving the status of motherhood became a way to improve the status of society in 1896 when "a founder of the National Congress of Mothers (which in 1924 became the PTA) linked the lack of rights and dignity of mothers to the poor quality and character of national life."

Women may have been largely powerless beyond their own four walls in those early years, but they used what authority they had to get what they needed. In fact, it was the mobilization of women on behalf of mothers that launched the human welfare legislation that finally took off during the Depression, when these kinds of social policies became a priority for both genders. (Unlike Europe, where welfare policies were often constructed around "paternal notions" such as workers' pensions, America's welfare state was constructed around "maternal" programs meant to protect mothers and families.) Beyond the obvious policy contributions by our early reformers, they shifted the "cultural norms of authority" by making the values of motherhood a public value—the expertise in home and family, transformed for the public good. Motherhood was viewed as "community service."

Their example has been followed by legions: In the 1970s, very brave women formed the Madres de Plaza de Mayo and began a vigil that helped take down Argentina's military junta when they circled the plaza every day for years, drawing attention to the disappearance of their children and thousands of others whose fates were unknown. The largest mobilization to end gun violence in America culminated in the Million Mom March in Washington in 2000. The creators of that march must certainly have looked to Mothers Against Drunk Driving (MADD), which started as a loosely assembled group of brokenhearted mothers. MADD is now the largest crime victims' assistance organization in the world, with more than three million members and supporters. Since its inception in 1980, alcohol-related traffic deaths have declined 43 percent.

Our undisputed strengths of family and community have been our motivators for public service. Representative Jan Schakowsky (D-IL) got her start protesting improperly labeled foods in local grocery stores. Senator Barbara Mikulski (D-MD) joined a group that was trying to stop a highway from destroying two important Maryland neighborhoods. The frustrations of the fight made her realize she'd rather open doors from the inside, so she took another road and became the first woman senator elected in her own right.

In the absence of role models and expectations that they should be leaders, and defying the odds that they could make a difference, these women across two centuries *claimed* their authority. At the present time, a trio of women governors elected in 2002 have broadened that reach by laying claim to issues normally reserved for men, bridging the gap in style and substance, successfully assuring voters they could be both tough and caring.

Governor Jennifer Granholm of Michigan, a former state attorney general, became "Jenni the giant-slayer" when she defeated both popular House minority whip David Bonier and former Democratic governor James Blanchard in the primary. Her platform: prescription drug programs, more jobs through attracting high-tech companies to the state, and corporate responsibility. She did it with fighting language, as befits a crusading attorney. After winning the primary, she vowed to "take back this state. We're going to do it for our parents, we're going to do it for our children [she's a mother of three], we're going to do it for everyone who has been excluded." The *New York Times* described her as alternating between "sincere whispers and dynamic declarations" and as offering "a fierce handshake followed by a soft shoulder touch."

She defeated her Republican opponent, Dick Posthumus (an unfortunate name, since he came to be known as Dead Man Running), by portraying herself as a hard-nosed leader still attached to progressive issues. In her state-of-the-state address, she referred to her election platform on the economy, jobs, and terrorism. And with a Kennedyesque flourish combined with a dash of woman, she said, "Life's most dazzling victories dawn when imagination finds a way they said couldn't be found. And the sweetest of all victories arise when those thought to be adversaries, together lead to a higher ground." It's a shame she can never make a state-of-the-union address unless we change the Constitution; she was born in Canada.

Governor Kathleen Sebelius, a former two-term insurance commissioner of Kansas, went right to her strength when she pitched herself as the health-care candidate. And because she had credentials from a job normally held by a man, she also got taken seriously on other "male" issues as well: law and order, safety and security, drugs and terrorism. Governor Janet Napolitano of Arizona, like Granholm a state attorney general, built on her leadership credentials as a tough prosecutor with a promise to pursue drug dealers and corporate polluters.

These three women brought powerful voices to public office by addressing nontraditional issues for women and insisting that they themselves be taken seriously. They overcame perceived weaknesses and managed to keep their strengths as women all the while. They authorized themselves, honoring their abilities and values, and then brought the voters along with them.

Authority for All

These campaigns are perfect illustrations of what is possible if women remember who they are and what they know, and then act on it; but every little edge counts, and it doesn't hurt to know a few tricks. During the White House Project's dial-testing study, where we showed real political ads used in governors' races, we also showed ads of our own making, with professional actors, to see if we could determine what worked. We confirmed what female candidates and their advisers suspected: Women can't present themselves in the same way men do and still be seen as authoritative. Here's what the women had to do to make it with the viewers:

1. Wear formal clothing, like a tailored suit and blouse. The rolled-up sleeve, out-on-the-range look did not translate into governor material, nor did the frilly look.

2. Use active language coupled with issues not ordinarily associated with women, like crime or the economy.

3. Use an impressive backdrop related to how you want to be seen, whether it's behind a desk or in front of the statehouse.

4. Discuss your credentials because the voters will require proof of your competence.

We distributed our research to every campaign where a woman was running for governor, mayor, or Congress, hoping it would help. We also gathered a group of businesswomen, introduced earlier, and they heavily identified with the plight of the candidates. One highly placed woman in the financial industry called me a month later to say she had incorporated the four points of advice into a corporate presentation. Supposedly, the occasion was dress-down, but she wore a business suit. She made sure there was a podium in the room to formally confer her authority. She monitored her language, keeping it active, and began with material that proved her competence. She said she had rarely had such a successful experience.

With a little help from us, this business executive changed the rules of engagement. And that's what it takes to break down barriers and change perceptions: giving each other a leg up whenever we can by rewriting the rules. In fact, as Gail Evans says in her new book, *She Wins, You Win,* it is vital that we play on the women's team—talking, planning, and collaborating to improve the situation for everyone. We stand a rung down because we don't band together, like men do, to create the power we need to move up. Evans proposes "a new strategy to advance our careers as a whole"—to become rainmakers for other women.

We need this strategy so we can counteract centuries of leading without authority. Interestingly, though, it has prepared us for the authority to lead, forcing us to think out of the box, to build consensus, to bring people together across communities. Harvard professor Ronald A. Heifetz explains that it's possible to lead "from the foot of the table," but it "requires trust, respect, and moral force in order to sustain progress . . . [The leader] may need people across boundaries to believe that she represents something significant, that she embodies a perspective that merits attention."

Gloria Steinem did it before she was a feminist icon. She gained both positional and moral authority, amassed from decades of travel and conversation throughout America as she organized the modern women's movement. Like the leaders Heifetz describes, Steinem had no choice but to work within and across communities, teaching and being taught, using her ability to place her struggles "in the context of the day's dominant values and concerns," working toward change by casting the net wide and deep.

Margaret Sanger, whose collaboration with others brought us the birth control pill, is another leader whose effectiveness came from touching the experiences of other women. Similarly, Eve Ensler's continuing dramatic success with *The Vagina Monologues* results from bringing the issue of violence against women straight into communities, allowing both genders to talk safely as victims and perpetrators.

These three leaders wrote extensively. One used theater. Another founded Planned Parenthood. They enlisted an army of participants, knowing they needed numbers to ensure permanent change. The American women's movement rose from old-fashioned organizing at kitchen tables with no money and little power, yet it birthed institutions like women's centers and domestic violence shelters, and provided a basis by which women can lead as it paved the road to formal positions of authority.

Getting to that formal authority will require a woman-by-woman guerrilla war, but you don't have to commit to hours of working toward social change to see tangible results. The effort can be as simple as introducing another woman to the boss with all the authority she deserves. It can be an informal meeting to share information. It can come in the form of a note of thanks, a note of praise, a note of support for a woman seeking a promotion. It can be spoken recognition of a woman's idea in a meeting, or recognition of a male ally. It can even be a conversation around the breakfast table, where we talk with the next generation about a new set of imperatives. But it must be consistent and persistent, and it has to involve *every* woman, making it safe by the magnitude of its numbers.

Consider the strategy of 250 women from Pittsfield, Massachusetts, in the November 2003 election. It started in a discussion between two of them, which led to the creation of an organization called WHEN (Women Helping Empower Neighborhoods, which was more tactful than its original name, We've Had Enough Nonsense). The women were motivated by an embattled female mayor and a dysfunctional city council of eleven white men whose televised antics at meetings were deemed "the best sitcom on TV." This image of the city fueled its inability to attract new business or to take care of the business at hand (like improving schools). The WHEN founders knew "that adding female voices to the council would help bring a less polarized political climate to Pittsfield."

The women educated themselves about the political process and built a woman-by-woman campaign. They recruited female candidates, held fund-raising coffees, and offered services tailored to the woman candidate: babysitting, home-delivered dinners, and after-school transportation both during the race and afterward for those who won. "Probably only a women's group would think of something like that," said Tricia Farley-Bouvier, a thirty-eight-year-old mother and one of three WHEN-endorsed council candidates to win (the female mayor lost). Next time: The group intends to recruit people of color to diversify the council even more.

Leadership consultant Shifra Bronzick reminded me that it's very hard to motivate women if they think the agenda is selfish or narrow, such as pushing themselves up the chain of command. We have been socialized to believe that a voice for personal gain is not a voice worth hearing, that our focus must always be outward toward helping others get what they need. That is why women blend so easily into social change movements. Movement goals are often "keeping someone alive," which creates a fuel of burning outrage. But, Bronzick says, how do you create this same outrage for just the loss of women's voice?

She is so right. We need trumpeting change, like the leaves of fall—a way to show our colors, to authorize women's voices, to remind ourselves that leaves need branches, that branches need trunks. A good start: Become trustworthy voices for each other, refusing to allow diminishment, fighting invisibility, reminding each other that we *are* experts, Your Honor. "Turn to your sisters for support," says Kimberly Otis, president and CEO of Women & Philanthropy. "It's a moral imperative."

4

AMBITION

Raise your hands. Raise your voice. Be ambitious. Don't take no for an answer. The world would be a better place if more women were running it, and so long as that is true, then ambition in women should be celebrated as a gift to all of us.

—*Susan Estrich,*
author and professor,
University of Southern California

Ambition in men is an expectation and a virtue. In women, it can be a kiss of death, guaranteeing isolation, ending relationships (personal and professional), pushing entire families into therapy, and making even the most self-assured CEO wonder what she was thinking.

Ambitious men anoint themselves for positions of power. They can be as diverse as magazine publisher Steve Forbes, conservative activist Alan Keyes, and tire magnate Morrie Taylor, all of whom ran for president without embarrassment. Men act with bald certainty of the right to ask, if not the right to win. And they get taken seriously, even when they shouldn't.

It's not that men don't have to manage their ambition. Obviously, any man who threatens his boss might find himself unemployed. The difference is that although men have to *manage* their ambition, women have to *mask* theirs. House Minority Leader Nancy Pelosi is a good example. Here is the story of her rise to power, told in an article in *Elle* just before the 2002 election: "The tale of how she became a congresswoman, for example, contains not a single reference to her own aspirations to have and wield clout. As the story goes, Pelosi transformed herself, reluctantly, from behind-the-scenes party functionary to front-line politician because she'd made a promise to a dying friend. The story, as it happens, is true. It is also so brilliantly non-threatening that it could have been invented by a team of image-honing consultants." Once in Congress, she loved the job, but says, "I never craved it."

Here's a woman who said she had no early ambition, but the minute she got power, the press put her in her place anyway. A 2003 article in *The American Prospect* talks of how Wesley Pruden, editor in chief of the *Washington Times,* called her "the Democrats' new prom queen," conservative columnist Cal Thomas said liberals like Pelosi represent the "Fidel Castro wing of the Democratic Party," and the *National Review* "dubbed her 'a latte liberal.'" Even normally even-handed Bill Keller, former columnist for the *New York Times* and now its executive editor, named Pelosi a member of Congress we would be better off without. Her sin, according to Keller: raising money for her colleagues (which *is* a job of a party leader).

Successful women often have to spin their ambition so they don't appear too unladylike. Shelly Lazarus, chair and CEO of Ogilvy & Mather Worldwide, talked in a 2001 *New York Times* article of her blend of public and private life, information that would probably hit the cutting room floor in an article about a male executive (if the questions were even asked). An *O* magazine piece, describing the *Times* article, talked of Lazarus's "memories of romantic liaisons with her future husband and family ski trips without her cell phone; her toy-strewn office and a particular affection for frogs; her determination to 'never take myself too seriously.' Here was a gentle female CEO even a business competitor could love." And, the article asks, "Do women still need to soft-sell their ambition with self-deprecation and a nurturing style?"

The answer is yes. For now, that's the only way women can be accepted as corporate and political leaders. Those who don't succumb to the soft sell may be denied the ultimate reward.

Case in point: the feisty, hard-selling Bella Abzug, a congressional champion of liberal causes who served nobly and brilliantly in the 1970s. If she had been a man, she would have been President Lyndon B. Johnson. She was just as pushy and in your face, just as committed to a Great Society. But the style of Johnson, now the stuff of legend, caused Abzug to be marginalized. She might have made a fabulous president, but we'll never know. A cartoon that appeared shortly after her death in 1998 said it all: A chunky woman in an oversized hat arrives at the pearly gates and pushes them over, stomping her way into heaven with a suitcase in her hand. "Welcome, Ms. Abzug," says St. Peter as she blows by without a second look.

It's no different at the corporate level. Deborah C. Hopkins, now chief operating officer at Citigroup and "one of the most media-scrutinized" of U.S. women executives, was dismissed as chief financial officer at Lucent Technologies just a year after she joined in 2000. She came "with a spectacular track record and, it was suggested, had accomplished the goals for which she was hired." "Her departure," according to the *New York Times,* "had less to do with her performance than with her personality." She worked hard and focused on her career, but the *Times* also quoted colleagues as saying she was "too impatient," "straightforward," "aggressive," "demanding," words that turn grudgingly positive when applied to men.

Often it takes no more than simple success to cause a backlash. Mellody Hobson of Ariel Capital Management—and a regular financial commentator on ABC's *Good Morning America*—was surprised to hear that a female friend of her company's male chair—and a very successful woman in her own right—had intimated to him that she was not "a fan of mine." The chairman was surprised, and he challenged his friend, "I'm kind of amazed because you've never really spent any time with Mellody. What is it about her?" The answer: "She's so ambitious." To Mellody's delight, the chairman didn't stop there: "If she were a man, would it still bother you?" The woman conceded that she would have to think about that.

The Appropriate Ambitions

"Show me a woman without guilt and I'll show you a man."

That old saw is one of my favorites, since I identify so heavily with it, never more than when I had ambition and five young children at home. Like all women in that situation, I was living a double life, feeling burdened and guilty about both, walking the plank of impossibility as I tried to be a good mother and a good worker. I frequently heard that familiar internal tape looping over and over: "When I'm at work, I'm often thinking about what's not done at home. When I'm at home, I'm aware of what's not done at the office."

Not all ambitions are created equal, and for women, two are unquestioned: wife and mother. These roles, of course, harken back to tradition. Any ambition beyond them can cost us because it is expected to come in addition to, and behind, the other two. If it doesn't, it can produce societal suspicion and boatloads of guilt. It's different for men; marriage and parenthood are "extra" ambitions, coming second to the prime directive of work. Men, after all, are culturally expected to be breadwinners.

The daily expectations of women with both a career and family come with consequences. If we drop the ball, the children might not be fed, the house might be filthy, our aging parents might fall while we're working, our husbands might get tired of us and find other women. Try as we might to do it all well, we often can't, which leads to the national pastime of mother blaming. My youngest daughter once told me that she overheard an airplane conversation so scathing about mothers that if she hadn't already loved me, she would have loved me then just to balance the negativity.

No one in recent history has paid a more unfair and more painful price for ambition than Hillary Rodham Clinton. She started her career as our national Rorschach test in the spring of 1992, during her husband's first quest for the presidency, when she responded to criticism of her law career by saying: "I suppose I could have stayed home and baked cookies and had teas." The shock wave nearly knocked her off her feet.

This ambitious, brilliant Wellesley- and Yale-educated lawyer, a partner in a powerful Arkansas firm, did not fit either the tradition or the image of a first lady. She seemed too much the politician herself and too little the politician's wife, and she was immediately stereotyped for it. By September 1992, near the end of the campaign, the *Times* noted that at least twenty articles in major publications had already compared her to Lady Macbeth, "a grim role model for political wives." When the *Times* polled voters, it found that many "viewed Mrs. Clinton as a behind-the-scenes manipulator who was the real power behind a pliant husband."

It didn't stop after the election: Military officials hung her picture in a Pentagon briefing room, captioned THE COMMANDER IN CHIEF. Shortly after his inauguration in 1993, President Clinton named her head of a committee to examine the nation's health-care system, "the most powerful official post ever assigned to a First Lady." Bill Clinton put this trust in his wife at the beginning of an eight-year administration; for Hillary Clinton it was undoubtedly too soon. The mission was complex and layered, and having her lead the charge made it even more treacherous. The initiative failed for a number of reasons, but one of them was surely having a first lady with public power (Nancy Reagan and Barbara Bush wielded theirs closer to the pillow). In her best-selling book *Living History,* Clinton says that neither she nor the president understood "the resistance [she] would meet as a First Lady with a policy mission."

In the end, it wasn't really about her. As Gloria Steinem said, "She's pioneering in public an issue that is at least as important in the long term as any of the issues considered political in the conventional sense, and that is an equal relationship between a man and a woman."

In a 1994 editorial in the *New York Times* entitled "Let Hillary Be Hillary," Joyce Purnick asks: "I wonder what this nonsense about cookies and pastels does to a bright, well-educated woman who has an established legal career? I wonder, too, what it is in the American psyche that wants its political wives to be Stepford Wives, fantasy femininity."

To the detriment of America, Hillary Clinton backed away from public policy after her failure at health care. To the benefit of America, her ambition was shelved only temporarily—she ran for senator of New York in 2000, and she won. Now she has the permission (and the title) she needs to go the distance. An added plus: Her daughter, Chelsea, is now grown and on her own, so she doesn't carry the stigma of the absent mother.

In many ways, fear of women's ambition, when it strays beyond the roles of wife and mother, is a fear of our desire, of our wanting. The resistance to women as leaders stems from an assumption that, were women given the chance, we would climb right up the ladder and away from men and children, authoring a life squarely at odds with our maternal mandate. So society limits our choices, providing little support in the workplace and making it tremendously difficult to have both a career and family. The lid is tight, and we are kept in our place by a system that refuses to create the means by which women can lead.

Even if some support exists at work, it is extremely difficult to have a career, a home, and a family simultaneously unless you have a spouse who rides shotgun. It can tend to be a "choiceless choice," as author and cultural anthropologist Mary Catherine Bateson calls it—the idea that you can have it all but you can't have it all at once. Three major research organizations—Families and Work Institute, Catalyst, and the Boston College Center for Work & Family—completed a study in 2002 called *Leaders in a Global Economy: A Study of Executive Women and Men*. The statistics are striking:

- 74 percent of women have a spouse or partner with a full-time job; 75 percent of men have a spouse or partner at home.
- 18 percent of women (versus half as many men) delayed marriage or commitment to "manage both their careers and their personal lives."
- 35 percent of women delayed having children for their careers, versus 12 percent of men. In the executive ranks, 90 percent of men have kids, compared to 65 percent of women.

These statistics support what young women say about their lives: They sometimes have to delay their ambition—or "stop out"—pulling away from a career to tend to home and hearth, resuming it later. More men and more institutions are making accommodations, but they are tinkering around the edges, not doing enough to really make a societal difference. And women, socialized to stifle their dreams, sometimes find it hard to ask for what we need.

"Mean Girls" and Other Youthful Patterns

It is not just society that guarantees we keep our ambitions in check; we also require it of one another, especially when we're young. Most recently, this phenomenon has been labeled "mean girls." It has been on the cover of the *New York Times Magazine;* columnists have written about it; books have been published on the subject; a movie produced by Lorne Michaels of *Saturday Night Live* fame is planned. The central idea: Girls can be just as nasty as boys when it comes to torturing "outsiders." This thesis has been hailed as positive symmetry, proof that the sexes are equal. In truth, there's nothing equal about this hostility, and it marks the beginning of women's lifelong struggle with ambition.

When boys are mean, they are expressing their *power;* when girls are mean, they are expressing their *lack* of power. Boys patrol the boundaries of the masculine, punishing those who do not measure up, bullying other boys into a definition of "manhood" that few can (or should) live up to. Girls patrol the boundaries of the feminine, ridiculing those who stray from the traditional female means of power—beauty and attachment to boys—a definition of womanhood that radically reduces their self-worth.

These girls react to their lack of power by controlling what they can: other girls. The power of many young girls continues to be derived from the boys they hang out with, and the bump it gives their popularity. In the years that follow, as they grow, far too many continue to hitch their star to a man, whose success or failure can determine their status. Ultimately, their ambition is to *please* men, not to *lead* them, even if their leadership abilities are stronger than the men around them.

"It's not testosterone, but privilege," says author and professor Michael S. Kimmel, an expert on men and masculinity. "In adolescence, both boys and girls get their first real dose of gender inequality: girls suppress ambition, boys inflate it."

This inequality becomes especially apparent in the male arenas of math and science, where girls undervalue their abilities. Because girls don't think they can make it in these fields dominated by men, only the strong among them tend even to try. Consequently, those who go the distance are truly gifted, resulting in high grades for each individual girl and a higher mean score for girls in general. For boys, says Kimmel, it's a different story. Their false bravado tends to make them "overvalue their abilities, to remain in programs though they are less qualified and capable of succeeding." Boys stick it out when they shouldn't, pulling down the scores of *all* boys.

It is no wonder that men wake up in the morning and ask themselves if they should run for president, while women need a drum roll and a draft before they even begin thinking about it. This point is underscored in a 2001 book—*Who Runs for the Legislature*—written by three political scientists. Their study found that 37 percent of male candidates polled said it was their own idea to run for office, compared to only 11 percent of females; 37 percent of women said they hadn't seriously considered it until someone else brought it up, but for men, it was half that number at 18 percent.

I resemble this study. In 1983, I ran for city council in Des Moines. I had a heart full of untapped political ambition, but I only got into the race when a friend already serving on the council swore she'd resign if I didn't join her. I was thrilled she called; I never would have entered on my own. There was a score of men in the primary, and they were tough. I had to have ambition and a fierce determination to win. Luckily I had both, and I needed them to deal with the daily thrills and disasters of a political race.

Most memorable was a ride in a small plane where an opponent piloted us through a storm while a male colleague tried to convince me to get out of the race. I advanced to the primary against this same man. One particularly special morning, I opened the paper to see that every male member of the city council had signed an ad opposing me and supporting him. In the end, I won. Without my passionate desire to serve, I probably would have dropped out early.

I wish I had had the encouragement (and the "courage" embedded in that word) to start earlier in politics. The earlier you tap that ambition, the further you get. According to a 2003 study by the Eagleton Institute of Politics at Rutgers University, called the *Young Elected Leaders Project,* half of the top U.S. elected officials—governors, senators, and representatives—held their first office at age thirty-five or younger. The project also looked at historical figures and found that twelve of the nineteen presidents who served in the twentieth century were under thirty-five when they first ran for office.

Of today's young political leaders, 86 percent are men and 81 percent are white. They are highly educated, and nearly a third of them had a relative who also served. This is quite a pipeline issue for women and people of color. The survey also proves the point about encouragement for women: Almost half of the men "self-started," but only 28 percent of the women said they struck out on their own initiative. Half of the women had been "encouraged;" but 22 percent had to be "persuaded," as opposed to 14 percent for men. The good news is that once in office, young women are just as ambitious as young men. The bad news is, they are only 14 percent of the group.

The study identified a starting point for action if we want to get more young women into politics: college. When in high school, equal numbers of the young men and women said they participated in governance, but when they got to college, the gap widened considerably—42 percent of the young men participated, as compared to only 19 percent of young women. In a 2000 White House Project survey, *Pipeline to the Future,* with a research base of six hundred women and two hundred men between the ages of eighteen and twenty-four, the men acknowledged they knew it was more difficult for women to step forward and run for office. As one young man said, "They might not even want to try. They [would] feel like a minority." These young men grew up in a society that expected them to run. They see themselves able to do any job; if they are elected, they fully expect to be able to figure it out, even if they have no previous background to draw upon.

In contrast, young women would feel on rocky ground if elected, unsure they could do the job well, needing mentors to demystify it. In France, after parity was voted in the early nineties and women candidates were sought to run, all the females on the list of possible legislators asked if there was a place they could go to learn the job. Not a single man ever asked such a question.

Ambition can also be fueled among groups not traditionally represented. Our same White House Project study found that while those women most ready to run are young, white, and college educated, a larger group of African Americans, Latinas, women without college degrees, and young mothers would also step forward if given information, exposure to opportunities, and good mentoring. If we can provide these tools, we have a ready-made next generation of diverse political recruits.

Young women with ambition do not just motor ahead and damn the torpedoes. They want to become public servants and titans of industry but—as law professor Derrick Bell says in his new book, *Ethical Ambition: Living a Life of Meaning and Worth*—they also want to know about choices they "will have to make as they gear up to pursue individual success in a competitive marketplace." How much unfairness will they experience? What price will they pay for integrity, especially in the business world? How do they fully realize their ambition without losing their own identities?

In my travels I have heard these questions over and over, but I've also heard a nascent ambition from young women, and a knowledge that helping to create public policy could change their lives and strengthen their communities. They're just not sure they want to do what they see as necessary to get there and to stay there. One young woman in the pipeline study captured the concern: "If you have values or morals, you're not going very far in politics." We need to change the risk/reward ratio that many view as an insurmountable barrier to entry. If we can increase the number of women in power at the highest level, we can turn the system inside out, creating the atmosphere we need to attract a new generation, and a new gender, of leaders.

Safety Zone

Men know full well that there is safety and power in numbers. Women, however, still work in isolation most of the time, and it is deadly difficult for us to say, "I deserve" or "I want." Consequently, as we've seen in the statistics on political candidates, we often need a shove from behind to get us to the microphone. If it's someone else's idea, it's easier to swallow, since we don't have to seem personally ambitious.

This was evident during the White House Project's 1999 straw poll of women who could be president. Our research showed that Americans would be willing to vote for women if they knew who was out there, so we thought we'd show them. A communications scholar prepared a list of the hundred most powerful women from business, government, education, the military, and advocacy, which we then winnowed to twenty names. The resulting nonpartisan ballot initiative was introduced in *Parade* magazine in September 1998, and was also offered on the Internet, through a 900 number, and in five other magazines: *People, Glamour, Essence, Latina,* and *Jane.* Ballots were distributed by hand in California, Colorado, Florida,

Georgia, Illinois, Iowa, Massachusetts, Michigan, New Hampshire, and New York. We wanted the public to see these amazing "candidates" from a variety of sectors, races, and regions, and to vote for five women of their choice. Our voters were asked to select women based on demonstrated leadership qualities, not political beliefs.

This was not partisan political business as usual, and it made some of my savvy friends nervous. They also warned that the women we chose would not want to be on the list because they'd be embarrassed, not wanting to be seen as ambitious. They insisted we ask permission before naming them. Better to ask forgiveness than permission, so we selected the candidates, printed the ballots, then made the calls. The reaction was overwhelmingly positive: Every woman understood the cultural importance of what we were doing.

The initiative was a great success, both in voter participation and in the leaders it revealed. More than one hundred thousand Americans voted, and the results were published in *Parade* magazine in February 1999. Among the top vote getters: Hillary Rodham Clinton; Elizabeth Hanford Dole; Senator Dianne Feinstein (D–CA); Lt. General Claudia J. Kennedy (the three-star head of U.S. Army intelligence at the time); then Governor Christine Todd Whitman of New Jersey; Ann Fudge (then president of Kraft Food's Maxwell House and Post divisions); and Dr. Mae C. Jemison, first African-American woman in space. Among others on the ballot: Wilma P. Mankiller, former principal chief of the Cherokee Nation; Judith Rodin, president of the University of Pennsylvania; and Marian Wright Edelman, founder and president of the Children's Defense Fund.

We did get a few calls—from women wanting to know why *they* weren't on the list. (We did not select candidates running for office that year so that we would not appear to be endorsing anyone, which left some powerful women off the ballot.) I considered these calls a triumph for well-placed ambition.

Getting this A-list of names before the American voting public was one goal of the poll. The other was to create a safety zone, allowing these women to express presidential ambitions (presuming they had any) without having to actually say it first themselves. Elizabeth Dole, soon to become a candidate herself, got on board: "The time is ripe for a woman president. There are many women who are prepared." Hillary Clinton said, "A young girl interested in public service can be told with a straight face that she, too, could grow up to be president." Lt. General Kennedy announced, "There is every possibility that I would run for elective office. . . ." Within two years she retired from the army and explored a bid for a senatorial seat in Virginia. Senator Feinstein spoke of "the stamina, the staying power, the determination, and the enthusiasm" it would take, and Governor Whitman said she expected "to see a woman on the ballot in 2000." It wasn't herself, as some suspected it might be, but each of these women got to express ambition, and some acted on it.

We also wanted to initiate a cultural shift through the sheer volume of women, letting the country get used to a critical mass of available and viable female candidates. It was not an accident that we used the vehicle of the presidency to highlight the need for numbers of women in power. The achievement of winning this office—or at least having many women try to reach for that brass ring—represents a monumental shift in power sharing. But let us not forget while in pursuit of the mountaintop that there are scores of feeder positions, large and small, that could be filled by worthy women. That alone, if accomplished, would forever alter the dynamics of decision making.

Women Helping Women Help Everybody

Everyone knows at least one woman who should be urged to follow her dream, a woman who is utterly capable of being more than she is if only she were given encouragement. We need to find her and feed her ambition. Don't wait for the culture to change. Change it yourself by helping others to step forward. As a woman put it in the Wellesley study on women's leadership, "Most of the guys who are doing things didn't wait to be asked. They either moved to the front of the room and raised their hand or they stood beside someone, tugged on their coattail and said, 'I'm willing, I'm able, I'm interested.'"

No one understood this issue more fully than the brilliant Eleanor Roosevelt. In 1933, the first year of FDR's presidency, she wrote and published a book called *It's Up to the Women*. The title was both a challenge and a forecast. Eleanor was never elected to public office, but her vast work as Franklin's legs had taught her a lesson. As she put it, "Only women in power would consider the needs of women without power." To make sure that women have a fair shake at the American dream, women would have to make it to the top, stay there, and look after one another. Without the leadership of women, nothing would change for women—or men. It was an audacious, ambitious prospect, driven by duty and conviction, and it informed all of ER's future endeavors.

It also proved to be true. Women's presence in state legislatures and other state-level elected offices, as we have seen, is closely associated with the adoption of woman-friendly policies. The 2002 *Leaders in a Global Economy* report, discussed earlier, also points out the power of female-to-female mentoring: When women have another woman as the most helpful person in their rise to power, they are more likely to reach the highest reporting levels of a company.

In his recent best-selling book, *Good to Great,* Jim Collins studied companies to determine why they excelled. He found that the best among them had CEOs (all men) who were fiercely ambitious for their work, not for themselves—just like Eleanor Roosevelt so many decades ago.

Acting "As If"

Members of the newest generation are quick to tell me how they have benefited from the work of my era, but they are equally as quick to point out they don't feel trapped by history, unable to speak to their ambitions. Justice Sandra Day O'Connor says in an interview about her new book, *The Majesty of the Law:* "Young women today have no concept about how hard it was for women to get the vote (in 1920) and how my generation couldn't get jobs. They just think, 'Oh, that was the Dark Ages.'"

Those Dark Ages are not so long ago, and our work then made possible the ability of the young now to act "as if," a culture bender with great power behind it. Their expectation of success is a good model.

I may suffer a feminist backlash for liking the *Legally Blonde* franchise, but we need more cultural models like the act-as-if character played by Reese Witherspoon. In the original movie she plays an important (yet imperfect) heroine dumped by a boy on his way to Harvard Law School who doesn't think she can keep up with the Ivy League. She takes him to the cleaners, getting into Harvard herself and succeeding. She is sexy; she has fun; she overcomes disappointment and remains smart and sharp-witted—and she cultivates her own power. In the movie she is confounded when other women put her down. Instead of fighting in their mud pile, she uses her girly clout honorably—yet still gets her way. And most important, she brings others along with her. On the downside, we accept her ambition because it comes in a fem package—physical and flirtatious—and because it is built around proving herself worthy of a man (in a nonthreatening way, of course). In the end, it no longer matters. She harnesses her power.

The original act-as-if girl is Hester Prynne in *The Scarlet Letter,* forced to wear that scarlet A. She refuses to name her lover, the local minister who, without the burden of public shame, grows esteemed in the community, a beloved voice of moral leadership. Then there's Prynne, who must display her sin for all to see. She is taunted even by the poor and hungry, whom she voluntarily clothes and comforts.

Nathaniel Hawthorne created a prophetic work that examines women's voice and place in community. We seldom remember its turnaround ending: Hester Prynne triumphs, transforming the burden of her scarlet A into a symbol of power. She not only survives as an outsider, she also finds strength in it; over time the townspeople grow to believe the A stands for "able" or "admirable." "She becomes a radical visionary, wishing to free both men and women from the injustice of paltry conventions." As Hawthorne writes of his character: "The world's law was no law for her mind." Freed from conformity—from the need to be a good woman—Prynne becomes a great woman who does good works.

Though women are no longer tagged as adulteresses, they are still valued in roles that limit the stage on which they could perform. Societal convention and perception keep all generations of women a little too close to home, holding the bullhorn away from a new voice in leadership. The trick is to take the confining A's of our lives— authority, ambition, ability, and authenticity—and turn them into strengths, as Prynne did.

Ambition, which has come to be defined almost entirely as a desire for economic success in a career, could mean so much more. Women in power have a chance to rewrite the meaning of the word, to have ambition for fairness, a just and safe world for our families and a more cohesive community acting for the common good. We can lead and redirect our desires not just toward consumption and personal success, but also toward a consuming, ambitious passion for connection, for interwoven webs of opportunity at work, and we need not forfeit who we are and whom we love in the process.

It takes so little to do it. You don't have to have an MBA or run for city council to foster ambition and fight the resistance. We too often say, "Women are our own worst enemies," because sometimes we don't join as we should in the workplace, supporting female leaders and bringing others along. It's a function of powerlessness, the view that there's precious little room at the top and the competition is fierce. True for now, but there's a way to change that: Get behind women whose values you trust and help them succeed, then make them accountable for mentoring the next level, for allowing others to realize their ambitions. Don't go through the door and close it behind you. If we hold one another back instead of pushing one another forward, we will most certainly stay stuck.

We must also learn to cultivate men as allies. There are plenty who, with encouragement, would rise to the occasion. It is important that we seek them out, not only for their help but also to keep them strong so they can mentor both genders, creating other support systems and even more allies.

But encouragement doesn't just happen at work. Scan the horizon for those you love and respect. Ask your best female friend what her ambition is or was. Encourage her to pursue it—helping, if you must, by forming a community of women for support. As payment, ask that friend to ask another friend the same question and then go on to support her ambition. And don't forget our daughters. Get behind them and encourage their most outrageous dreams, from the locker room to the boardroom to the Senate cloakroom—or the Oval Office. Let's start a chain letter to unlock the CEO in every female. Or perhaps the network anchor. Or the next president.

"Keep a really big dream," says Cathleen Black, president of Hearst Magazines. "You'll need it along the way."

5

ABILITY

BRING ME MEN.

*—From a stone arch that, until recently,
stood on the co-ed campus of the U.S.
Air Force Academy in Colorado*

Few would challenge the notion that women are as able as men, if given the same opportunities and training. We can be—and have been—scientists and diplomats, CEOs and athletes, astronauts and soldiers. But we also possess skills learned much closer to home: a collaborative style, community building with a focus on broader issues, a tendency to reach across lines of authority.

Motherhood, often used as an excuse to keep us down, is actually one of the best sources of our power. It is not only the place where our authority and ambition go unquestioned, but it is also a profession that breeds ability, and not just for stain removal. We are only now admitting that it is also respectable work with real economic value, even though it has not always been seen that way.

In her 2001 best-selling book, *The Price of Motherhood,* Ann Crittenden lays out early history: "As women's family labor lost status as 'work,' it was increasingly sentimentalized as a 'labor of love'. . .

Jeanne Boydston, the leading historian of the 19th Century domestic economy, argues that both husbands and employers enjoyed a free ride on wives' unpaid labor . . . Their activities enabled employers to pay extremely low wages, a factor that 'was critical to the development of industrialization in the antebellum Northeast'. . . . The reigning family myth—that men 'supported' women as well as children—prevented the great majority of women from seeing themselves as valuable economic players and equal marriage partners. They couldn't feel cheated of the fruits of their labor if they didn't believe that what they were doing *was* labor."

At the beginning of the twentieth century, women's economic value in the home was eroded further: Females actually moved to the other side of the balance sheet, becoming a cost. At the time, according to Crittenden, "The notion that women at home were 'dependents' had acquired the status of a scientific fact. The idea that money income was the only measure of human productivity had triumphed. With official blessing, husbands could consider wives not as economic assets but as liabilities. The theft was breathtaking."

Crittenden also makes the argument that mothers may have "the most important job in the world." Why? Because, as many economists assert, "human abilities are the ultimate front of economic progress." The nurturing role of mothers makes them among "the most important producers in the economy." Studies mentioned by Crittenden, a former economics reporter for the *New York Times,* estimates a realistic value of women's services at the middle manager level of $100,000 a year (though in one example, it was more than $500,000, a number derived by "adding up the median annual salaries of the seventeen occupations a mother is expected to perform, from child rearing, cooking, and cleaning to managing household finances and resolving family emotional problems.").

Anyone with that many skills should not only be paid for them but she should also find herself in demand in the workplace. Yet we have become like the Internet: Our basic services have been free for so long that it's hard for anyone to think about paying for them. Furthermore, though our services are free to others, they come at a price to us—what Crittenden calls the "mommy tax:"

- Inflexible workplaces that guarantee many women "will have to cut back in, if not quit, their employment once they have children. The result is a loss of income that produces a bigger wage gap between mothers and childless women than the wage gap between young men and women."
- Inequity in the event of a divorce, as the woman ends up in a much worse place than a spouse who has a career.
- A job that is not even defined as "work" by social policies. You are not considered a "full productive citizen" and as a family's primary caregiver, you are not eligible in your own right for Social Security credit.
- No unemployment or worker's compensation insurance as the primary parent.
- A job that is "the single biggest risk factor for poverty in old age."

We pay either way, in spite of the fact that the skills of mothering translate directly to good leadership. Some of the sixty prominent women who participated in the 2001 Wellesley College leadership study "identified a framework for understanding the roots and practices of leadership as emerging from mothering. The participants [who came from the top of sectors as diverse as education, nonprofit organizations, communications, and finance] spoke of mothering as both a training ground for leadership and a metaphor for describing leadership behavior . . . The majority of these leaders combined a strong focus on results with equal attention to the growth and development of the people surrounding them." And "the descriptions of nearly every woman's leadership practice included elements of the democratic, people-oriented style"—a style commonly associated with women. "Just as men have used military and sports metaphors to talk about their leadership, so women leaders . . . are talking about it from a decidedly female perspective by using female language." But it concludes, "Many of the traditional ways of talking and thinking about leadership can continue to mask the strengths women bring to their successful lives as leaders." The male-oriented definition, locked as it is in a command-and-control style, does not make room for women's way of leading through consensus.

The study's purpose was not to glorify motherhood, but to draw a parallel between the lives women lead in the home and the abilities honed there, and the powerful lives they could lead—and the good they could bring—beyond their own front yard.

Governor Mom

In spite of our insistence that work remain paramount for men, we still like our male leaders to be parents. It humanizes them and reassures us of their ability to love and nurture. Who can forget the Kodak moments (carefully staged) during the Kennedy presidency, all meant to soften the image of (and project virility onto) John F. Kennedy, a master stroke of public relations now that we know how ill he was in those years.

Would that it worked so well for women. Jane Swift, former

pregnant Republican governor of Massachusetts, was ordered in 2001 to rest in a hospital several weeks before she was due. Technology being what it was, Swift insisted she could easily run the state from bed. Her doctor agreed, saying her energy and stamina were "excellent." Certainly, her girth didn't lessen her ability to govern. But when she tried to conduct a governor's council meeting by speakerphone, the eight Democratic members questioned its constitutionality because she was not literally in the room. They voted, five to three, to ask the state supreme judicial court if Swift could conduct an official meeting by telephone. Ultimately the council decided to reverse its request to the court.

Maybe they remembered recent history and its different standard for men: President Ronald Reagan, nearly felled by an assassin's bullet in 1981, was hailed as a hero for ruling the nation from his sickroom. Women are no less brave. The vast majority, from Appalachia to Afghanistan, will never enjoy the luxury of a maternity ward, yet they have been known to work the fields until the moment of birth, stop to deliver the baby (themselves), then resume their other labor. The month before my fourth child was born in 1968, I was moving into a new home, wallpapering and painting, plus taking care of three children under five. When I heard the story of Jane Swift, all I could think was, what a piece of cake—running a state, with help, from a bed. Bring it on!

Brig. General Mary Ann Krusa-Dossin of the U.S. Marine Corps public affairs office was a military police operations officer when she became pregnant in 1979. She was immediately told she would be relieved of that post for the duration. Her Marine boss said he was concerned that, in her condition, she would not be seen as authoritative. Then-Sergeant Krusa-Dossin disagreed, knowing well her ability to command. She went through the pregnancy giving the same loud orders, which were dutifully obeyed. In fact, her Marines bonded with the baby like co-parents and almost insisted on naming it, proving that the general wasn't the only one suffering from stereotyping.

The thought that a mother might abandon her children for power and status deeply troubles Americans. In research released in 2001 by the Barbara Lee Family Foundation called *Keys to the Governor's Office,* voters said they are comfortable with male candidates having teenagers, but they prefer women to have adult children. "If she became governor and her kid got run over by a car and was in a wheelchair, she would be done," said a focus group participant. Interesting analogy, since a similar scenario created tremendous sympathy for Vice President Al Gore. As a senator from Tennessee, he kept vigil at the bedside of his son, who had been hit by a car.

In her 2000 race for governor of North Dakota, Heidi Heitkamp, Democrat and state attorney general, was asked how she would deal with her children. She replied, "The same way my male opponent will deal with his." That pretty much ended it, except she lost. Democrat Mary L. Landrieu of Louisiana has young children, and won the toughest and longest Senate race of 2002. And, of course, there's that famous pioneer Pat Schroeder, former Democratic representative from Colorado, who had to contend with motherhood and power in the 1970s, when the odds were stacked even higher against women (she said that the average contribution to her 1972 campaign was $7.50). Her unforgettable answer to the inevitable question, How can you be both a lawmaker and a mother: "I have a brain and a uterus, and I use both."

Dueling Polls

Americans show signs of gender schizophrenia, sometimes convinced women should rocket straight to the top, sometimes preferring them (and men) to stick to the stereotypes.

It looked like we were really getting somewhere when a Gallup poll conducted in January 2001 indicated that a majority of Americans (57 percent) believed the country would be better governed with more of us in political office. (In 1984, half that amount, or 28 percent, had agreed that women in government would improve it.)

Less than a year later, in November 2001, a RoperASW survey for the Ms. Foundation for Women delivered another message. Nearly six in ten Americans said they felt the sexes were naturally suited to different jobs: seven in ten said men were better plumbers, and women were better child-care workers. Significant numbers also said that working as a pilot, a CEO, or a politician was more a guy thing. Working as a stay-at-home parent, a nurse, or a flight attendant was more a girl thing.

Not even a year after that, the message switched back, and expanded. A RoperASW poll for the White House Project in the spring of 2002 found a majority of Americans comfortable with women at the top of most industries—over 90 percent felt we can lead large technology companies, major film studios, universities, financial institutions, law firms, newspapers, charities, and large retail organizations, as well as serve in Congress.

This about-face would be more exciting if it didn't come with a caveat. Apparently, these open-minded Americans who think we should be leaders blame our lack of advancement on their neighbors—76 percent expressed their *personal* comfort with a woman president, but they said they believe only 50 percent of *people* are comfortable with a female head of state. The tendency to let other people "say" what you yourself are uncomfortable saying is quite common in opinion polls. Another RoperASW survey, conducted for Deloitte & Touche in 2000, asked respondents to assess whether *most people* think a male or female president would perform better on specific issues. They are almost twice as likely to say that *most people* would put "more stock" in a man than a woman. Large majorities also said that *most people* think a man would perform better in foreign policy (70 percent), law and order (69 percent), governmental problems (63 percent), and the economy (58 percent). Women get higher marks in trustworthiness (89 percent) and honesty (88 percent).

What does this say? Does character matter less in the selection of leaders than, say, a degree in international relations? So many men have been elected president without any knowledge of or experience in major issues, including the economy and foreign affairs, yet they are perceived to be good at them (or at least to be quick studies) by virtue of their gender.

It's no better in Britain. The Tory parliament, which is only 8 percent female, can't seem to field women candidates, mostly because they don't think they're as good as men. In fact, the central office had to prove to the constituency parties that women have the same abilities. In 2003, they hired a psychologist to test the candidates, using "the interpretation of problems and queries to measure the intelligence, aptitude and personality traits," rating each candidate on "six 'competencies': communication skills, listening skills, intellectual skill, how they relate to others, their leadership motivational skills, and their political convictions." The men and women rated equally.

Americans, too, want and need proof that women have what it takes, especially when it comes to traditional "man's work." In the *Keys to the Governor's Office* study, we are told that "focus group participants wanted to see specific financial, crisis management and political credentials when evaluating whether a woman could handle the complexities of running a state. . . . In contrast, men were assumed to be qualified to lead their state if they had a résumé that simply listed positions of leadership and service." The study pointed out that "male voters, in particular, fear that a woman will not have the skill to manage her state's finances, especially in times of trouble, regardless of her previous business experience."

Again and again, women battle perceptions of what they can do, often based on gender. In the 1998 book *Why So Slow? The Advancement of Women,* by Hunter College professor Virginia Valian, we learn that even if a woman is at the head of a table, she is not automatically seen as, or treated as, a leader. In an experiment Dr. Valian showed college students a series of slides of five people at a table, one at the head and two on each side, then asked the students to identify the leader among them. When all the people at the table were of one gender, the answer was clear: Whoever sat at the head was the leader. If the groups were mixed and a man was at the head of the table, he was seen as the leader. However, in mixed groups, if a woman sat at the head, the students didn't automatically identify her as leader; half the time, they picked a man who sat in another spot. "The symbolic position of leadership [the head of the table] carries less symbolic weight for [women]," says Dr. Valian. And female students were as likely as males to respond in this way.

We are often hardest on ourselves. A friend who teaches labor relations at Rutgers University organizes each class into groups for a collective bargaining exercise, where over a period of weeks teams "negotiate" an agreement between students acting as union leaders and as employers. At the conclusion she asks each student to assign a grade to the whole group, to their individual teammates, and to themselves. Even when women had done more work, they tended to give themselves B's and the men in their group A's. The men, on the other hand, gave themselves and their group A's. The women also hung back and let the men take the lead—even when they weren't the best students—then did all the work in support of them. The job of recording secretary always fell to a woman, and usually the brightest one.

My friend asked the women to stay after class one day and then told them what she had observed, admonishing them to cut it out, "If you don't value your own work, no one else will. It's bad enough that society undervalues it." The women were surprised and sometimes tearful, but the next day the e-mails arrived: "Thank you. No one ever tells us this."

Women's War for Peace

Nowhere are women's abilities challenged as forcefully as they are in national and international conflict resolution, where war could be the inevitable outcome of a bad negotiation. I find this so frustrating because it is the single biggest factor keeping women from high political office. When we stop to think about the leadership qualities we truly need in the world, riddled as it is with armed rebellions and wars, the conclusion is starkly obvious: Send in some women.

I am thoroughly convinced that there will be no sustaining peace in any corner of the globe without able females to help lead the charge. This may be the most important contribution women in leadership would make, and it is a job for which our abilities are ideally suited. In the words of Haris Silajdzic, former co-prime minister of Bosnia and Herzegovina, "If we'd had women around the table, there would have been no war; women think long and hard before they send their children out to kill other people's children."

Yet as we have seen, polls indicate that men are trusted far more than women on foreign policy and on law and order. A few notable women from recent history have chipped away at the notion that we are inferior in this arena: Madeleine K. Albright, secretary of state in the Clinton administration, and Condoleezza Rice, national security adviser to President George W. Bush. But chipping away won't do it; we need many more women negotiating conflict in this world if we truly intend to stop war. We have been training for this job all our lives, negotiating home and community with empathy and a willingness to compromise—which seems to be part of the problem.

Ambassador Swanee Hunt tells how she got the idea for her Women Waging Peace program at Harvard, a program that advocates full participation of women in both formal and informal peace processes:

"When I was the ambassador [to Austria], Bosnia was right next door, and there was a terrible refugee flood into Austria. What I noticed quickly was that the 60 people who were sent up from Croatia and Bosnia for the [peace] negotiations were all men—even though there were more women PhDs per capita in the former Yugoslavia than in any country in Europe. It made me wonder why the warriors involved wanted to make sure there were no women.

"That question stayed in the back of my mind. After I left the State Dept. and came to Harvard, I asked some people at the U.N. why there were no women on the negotiating team in the African conflicts. A U.N. official told me: 'That's very clear. The warriors won't have them because they're afraid the women will compromise.' I thought: 'Bingo!' That is, after all, the whole point of negotiation." We are needed, as her organization points out, not only for our ability to compromise, but also because we bridge gaps more easily and we have our pulse on the community.

In an article from the 2001 May/June issue of *Foreign Policy* magazine, Ambassador Hunt and Cristina Posa (former judicial clerk at the UN International Criminal Tribunal for the former Yugoslavia and now an attorney at a New York law firm) outline the increasingly powerful roles that women are playing to create and sustain peace, driven not by gender fairness but by efficiency.

While most men come to the negotiating table directly
from the war room and battlefield, women usually ar-
rive straight out of civil activism and—take a deep
breath—family care . . . The idea of women as peacemakers is not political correctness run amok. Social
science research supports the stereotype of women as
generally more collaborative than men and thus more
inclined toward consensus and compromise. Ironically,
women's status as second-class citizens is a source of
empowerment, since it has made women adept at finding innovative ways to cope with problems. Because
women are not ensconced within the mainstream,
those in power consider them less threatening, allowing women to work unimpeded and "below the radar
screen." Since they usually have not been behind a ri-
fle, women, in contrast to men, have less psychological
distance to reach across a conflict line. (They are also
more accepted on the "other side," because it is assumed that they did not do any of the actual killing.)
Women often choose an identity, notably that of mothers, that cuts across international borders and ethnic
enclaves. Given their roles as family nurturers, women
have a huge investment in the stability of their communities. And since women know their communities,
they can predict the acceptance of peace initiatives, as
well as broker agreements in their own neighborhoods.

Webs of inclusion, empathy, collaboration, community and family focus: The abilities of women are ideally suited to maintain the
peace—making our presence a critical missing component among
today's ruling elite. It was one thing when warriors killed only one

another, but that nicety is disappearing. In a New York City speech for Save the Children in May 2003, philanthropist Teresa Heinz Kerry (wife of presidential candidate Senator John Kerry of Massachusetts) spoke of the difference in terms of civilian casualties between today's thirty-odd world conflicts and the wars of yesteryear. At the turn of the last century, she said, civilian casualties accounted for 5 percent of deaths; now they account for 90 percent. In other words, as Posa and Ambassador Hunt point out in their article, "Warfare has become 'inclusive'. . . so, too, must our approach toward ending conflict. Today, the goal is not simply the absence of war, but the creation of sustainable peace by fostering fundamental societal changes."

War is not the only threat to our security. In 1997, in an article for *Foreign Affairs* when she was a senior fellow at the Council on Foreign Relations, Jessica Tuchman Mathews (now president of the Carnegie Endowment for International Peace) put forward the notion of "human security." As she said, "Non-traditional threats . . . are rising—terrorism, organized crime, drug trafficking, ethnic conflict, and the combination of rapid population growth, environmental decline, and poverty that breeds economic stagnation, political instability, and, sometimes, state collapse." She points out that since the end of the cold war in the 1980s, there have been about one hundred armed conflicts worldwide. "Many began with governments acting against their own citizens, through extreme corruption, violence, incompetence, or complete breakdown, as in Somalia."

Because of these alarming trends, Dr. Mathews points out that the security of an individual doesn't necessarily derive from the security of the nation. Hence, "human security," the idea that "security be viewed as emerging from the conditions of daily life— food, shelter, employment, health, public safety—rather than flowing downward from a country's foreign relations and military strength."

These are the very issues to which women have been intimately connected for millennia, and they make us ideally suited to fix any lapses.

Mathews's hypothesis was borne out by three years of research (housed at the Rockefeller Brothers Fund) that was released in 2001 by the Aspen Institute and titled *A Women's Lens on Global Issues.* The report explores the values of American women and how these values could shape our involvement in the international arena.

The study identified a number of threats to global stability, including environmental degradation, economic development, human rights, and health-care issues such as AIDS. While both genders share "a commitment to international cooperation," women would act differently to get there. In the words of the study, females are more likely to:

- Believe nations need to work together.
- Support international programs that meet basic human needs—a "human security" agenda—and empower women.
- Emphasize diplomacy over military power.

You won't be surprised to find that women's core values on foreign policy are expressed in terms of a global neighborhood marshaling community forces for the common good. American women see the interconnections—they want the United States to be a good neighbor and a teacher, not a cop and a banker. Women don't want to remake others in our image; they want to help those in need through active engagement. To attend to global affairs, they feel, is to attend to U.S. affairs.

A new book titled *How Women Can Beat Terrorism* by Curt Weeden demonstrates "how women in the U.S., Europe and other developed nations . . . can move the world toward a more peaceful tomorrow."

Weeden believes that supporting women who live in parts of the world where they are "more often repressed than respected . . . offer[s] us our best chance of venting the buildup of socio-economic pressures that is hazardous to all of us." He isolates the "core" problems that breed terrorism as hopelessness, poverty, and overpopulation in parts of the world that cannot absorb it.

Weeden proposes we ask four key questions of candidates for national office:

- Will you support allocating at least 0.7 percent of your country's annual budget for helping developing countries combat poverty at the grassroots level?
- Do you agree that such grass-roots programs should be aimed at helping women wherever it is practical and possible?
- Will you assign the highest possible priority to curbing reproduction rates in those parts of the world already under stress because of population growth?
- Will you support signing the Convention for the Elimination of All Forms of Discrimination Against Women (CEDAW) [adopted by the UN in 1979; only a few countries haven't signed it, including the United States]?

Let's add the following question to his list for the 2004 election: Will you agree to put a critical mass of women in your new administration? If that happens, Weeden's questions are sure to be answered the way they should.

The United Nations Security Council issued a resolution in 2000 asking Secretary-General Annan to use more women in the field. Though the resolution is unenforceable, it has created a well-spring of women's activism with tangible results: UN peacekeepers were trained in both "gender sensitivity and the prevention of HIV and sexual violence" before arriving in Sierra Leone. UNIFEM, an organization affiliated with the UN that works on global women's issues, helped establish a peace delegation to Burundi composed of fifty women who recommended proposals to the mediator, former South African president Nelson Mandela; he adopted nineteen of them in the final agreement. A nationally televised debate, organized by women in the Democratic Republic of Congo (Zaire), lobbied for more women at the peace table there.

The European Parliament passed its own resolution that same year, urging members "to promote the equal participation of women in diplomatic conflict resolution; to ensure that women fill at least 40 percent of all reconciliation, peace-keeping, peace-enforcement, peace-building, and conflict-prevention posts; and to support the creation and strengthening of NGO's [nongovernmental organizations] (including women's organizations) that focus on conflict prevention, peace building, and post-conflict reconstruction."

In our own country, Congresswoman Eddie Bernice Johnson (D-TX) is leading a charge with her mantra, "No women, no peace." She sponsored a House resolution after September 11 that outlines the need for women to help in negotiations. The resolution, which has yet to pass, goes to the heart of women's community involvement, asking civic and women's groups to lobby for peace. In March 2002, she also launched A World of Women for World Peace, whose program allows international women to talk about alternatives to war. Why did Representative Johnson take it on? "It was incumbent upon me—not only as a member of Congress, but as a mother and a grandmother. . . ."

Woman Warriors

While women are peacemakers, they are also unacknowledged warriors. Though their contributions have historically been overlooked, nearly two million female war veterans have served the United States of America. From the American Revolution in the eighteenth century to Iraq in the twenty-first century, women have been present in every military conflict. "We're just like the guys. We're all going to be dodging bullets," says Lucita Warglo, a sergeant whose job is keeping runway lights and military camps powered in Iraq.

Today there are 200,000 active-duty women and 140,000 reserves. Women are one in seven of U.S. personnel in Iraq, yet only 33 women in the armed forces wore the stars of an admiral or general in 2002. One level down in rank, among colonels and captains, there is progress: Fifteen years ago, women made up fewer than 2 percent of this pipeline, but by 2000, it had shifted to 8 percent of the army, 10 percent of the navy, and 8 percent of the air force. And not a moment too soon. Female soldiers take just as many risks and pay just as steep a price in service to their country, and they should be rewarded with rank.

No one knows this better than a survivor of Desert Storm, army colonel Rhonda Cornum, who was shot, captured by the enemy, and sexually assaulted during her time as an Iraqi prisoner of war in 1991. Her quote, etched on a glass panel of the Women in Military Service for America Memorial in Washington, D.C., says it all: "The qualities that are most important in all military jobs—things like integrity, moral courage, and determination—have nothing to do with gender."

Tell it to the women at the U.S. Air Force Academy in Colorado. When called to duty, they fight just like the men, yet they risk a high price to get there—not from the enemy, but from their male classmates. More than 140 current and former cadets have filed complaints of sexual attacks at the academy in the last decade (81 of which were not investigated), leading to the dismissal of four top officers and the long-overdue removal of the inscription BRING ME MEN from a stone arch on campus. One woman who spoke up, and became a target for retribution, framed it in terms of ability: "It's the entire belief system, that women are inferior, and that's not so easy to change."

Lt. General Claudia Kennedy, now retired, was a top vote getter in the White House Project's straw poll. As the highest-ranking woman in army history and herself a whistle-blower on military sexual harassment, General Kennedy had this to say in the 2003 summer issue of *Ms.* magazine: "Widespread sexual harassment means the place is run like a gang, not like a business—and not like a cohesive fighting force. It means that loyalty within the group has replaced loyalty to the institution and its mission and what it stands for." A woman of towering integrity, General Kennedy stayed loyal to the institution by disclosing her abuse in 2000, when the army tried to put the very man who she said had abused her in charge of investigating harassment claims.

During the summer of 2003, the *Times* reported that a military panel had exonerated officials at the U.S. Air Force Academy in the handling of reported attacks. "Leadership did not avoid the issue," according to the air force's general counsel, Mary L. Walker. A recommendation: Assertiveness training (!) for first-year female cadets, who accounted for a majority of the complaints. The article mentioned no programs to deal with the aggression of male cadets, a major source of the problem.

Later in the summer the Defense Department released the results of a survey of 2003 female graduates—nearly 12 percent had either been raped or nearly raped during their time at the academy (the actual percentage is probably higher; 10 percent of women didn't answer the survey). Most of those who were attacked never reported the incidents, since victims were routinely punished while the men went free.

I've often wondered how those few women at our mostly male military academies hang on. A recent study by the University of California at Los Angeles may provide part of the answer: Women's brain chemistry makes us better able to handle stress. Previously, it was thought that stress triggered a "hormonal cascade" producing one of two responses: Stand and fight, or get the hell out of there. It turns out women might have a "larger behavioral repertoire" thanks to the release of the hormone oxytocin, which encourages us to "tend children and gather with other women."

Don't laugh. It's not what you think. When women act on that instinct, even more of the hormone is released, and it calms us down, lowering our stress level. Sorry, guys. It doesn't happen to you because men produce a ton of testosterone under stress, overpowering the good effect of their oxytocin. Our estrogen, on the other hand, appears to enhance it.

It played out even among the scientists who produced the study. "There was this joke that when the women who worked in the lab were stressed, they came in, cleaned the lab, had coffee, and bonded," said Laura Cousin Klein, one of the study's authors. "When the men were stressed, they holed up somewhere on their own."

Less scientifically than the study, Oxygen Media's chair and CEO, Geraldine Laybourne, simply wonders why so few have caught on to women's brain power:

> The sooner everybody understands the strategic importance of women's brains, the better off we're going to be. We may not be perfect, but we have this extraordinary prefrontal cortex. It enables us to think about

twelve to twenty topics at once. If you can combine that with the kind of driven, focused energy that's more associated with [men], you have a dynamite combination.

Resources in the future are going to be all about who deploys them with the least effort and the most success, and that's going to come from good strategic thinking. It's in women's capacity to be fantastic strategic thinkers. Instead, people say, "They're scattered, they're flighty, they think about one thing and then the other, they are more intuitive than they are analytical." Well, guess what? Eighty percent of all business decisions are based on intuition and twenty percent on facts, so you damn well better get a bunch of women in there.

Ready and Able to Create Change

Mathilde Krim took the stage at the 2003 National Women's Leadership Summit of the White House Project, reminding us how the acts of one woman can enable massive change. Dr. Krim has dedicated her life to increasing public awareness of AIDS, its causes, and its modes of transmission. In fact, she was in on the beginning of the fight to end this plague in the early 1980s, founding the first private organization fostering and supporting research on the disease, and issuing warning after unheeded warning about the health crisis. As chair of the American Foundation for AIDS Research (amfAR), she reminded our audience that seven years were lost while our country, in its homophobia, ignored the obvious, causing delays in research and guaranteeing countless deaths.

Catherine Muther, when she was head of marketing at Cisco

Systems in 1989, distributed buzzers to executives, which they could set off when they heard a sexist remark. She took money she earned with her good fortune to build Women's Technology Cluster, an incubator for women's technology ventures in that mostly male field.

Marsha J. Evans took her decades of naval experience (she retired as a rear admiral) and transformed it into a different kind of recruiting in her four years as national executive director of the Girl Scouts of the USA. Evans, now president and CEO of the American Red Cross, made sure that scouting was available to a diverse population of girls; one program, for instance, was designed for girls whose mothers are incarcerated.

You don't have to have a doctorate or stock options or a naval rank to spin the globe in another direction. In fact, those with the least access to resources often have the most access to ability and courage.

Denise King was diagnosed with HIV in 1995. She felt isolated by the secret as she moved through graduate school in social work in Albany, New York. "My first year of school, it felt like people could tell I had HIV just by looking at me. Every time the topic came up in class, it seemed like everyone was staring at me." Then she found Vanessa Johnson, of the Capital District African American Coalition on AIDS, another HIV-positive woman, confident and open, who urged her to join a leadership development program for other women like herself. The only requirement: Denise had to disclose her HIV status. She did, and instead of finding stigma within her school, she found support. She now works with Vanessa to end that stigma for others.

Lakita Logan, twenty, grew up and grew strong in Portland, Oregon, amid images of domestic violence, and amid racism in the public schools and the judicial system. While in a teen parenting class, she heard a lecture on self-defense by a member of Sisters in Action for Power. She joined, became a board member, and then the first teenage staff member, coordinating projects such as a successful public transit campaign to provide low-income students with subsidized bus passes. As she says, "I try to convey every day how important it is for girls and young women of color to speak out when decisions are made about our neighborhoods. Too often, it's the people who don't live here who make those decisions. We have a right to be at the table, too."

Staci Haines, a survivor of child sexual abuse, turned unease about the topic into action in San Francisco when she founded Generation Five, whose mission is to end all forms of child abuse within five generations. "What I realized," she said, "is that many people work on the healing aspects of sexual abuse, but no one was looking at how to end it."

Northern New Hampshire, with its scenic White Mountains, is not only a vacation paradise but also one of the most economically depressed regions in the country. With no public transportation and no industry beyond seasonal tourism, many residents are either unemployed or trapped in low-paying service jobs, leaving them isolated and unconnected to community. Enter Natalie Woodroofe and a few colleagues who started the Women's Rural Entrepreneurial Network to help low-income women develop business skills and build community through membership in the organization. "Community is clout," Woodroofe says. "When there are hundreds of you, people have to pay attention."

These women, all grantees of the Ms. Foundation for Women, took the resources of personal strength and community knowledge and turned them into permanent change—for themselves and for others. You don't have to quit your job or even volunteer in your off hours to exercise different muscles. Your contribution could be as simple as insisting, when others deny it, that motherhood is a hothouse for ability. You could set off your own internal buzzer, challenging sexism in the moment, or ask why women in your company never seem to land certain jobs. You could start a pipeline club to promote women's political careers. And what about you? Are you reticent about your own abilities? Do you apologize when you toot your own horn? Stop that behavior and go for the promotion, or speak up at meetings when you know you can answer the question. Or just urge others to do the same.

Often the small, incremental movements create the most change. The casual flapping of a butterfly in Brazil, if the air patterns are right, can change the weather thousands of miles away. If we interrupt even one entrenched pattern a day, we will create our own butterfly effect, changing the lives of women far beyond our own shores.

6

AUTHENTICITY

Don't compromise yourself. You are all you've got.

—*Janis Joplin*

In 1993, at the close of our very first Take Our Daughters to Work Day in New York City, a female executive at Brooklyn Union Gas addressed the girls in the company offices. A hand shot up with a question. It was the girl who had been assigned as her "daughter" for the day.

"I noticed your job was boring," the girl said.

"Maybe a little boring," the woman replied, a bit taken aback.

"Didn't you ever want to do something else?"

"Yes, I did."

"What did you want to do?"

"I wanted to be a singer," came the surprising answer.

"Well, sing me a song!"

And with that simple request, the buttoned-up executive belted out a Barbra Streisand standard, "The Way We Were."

I cried when I first heard that story, as do audiences who hear it from me. Without knowing it, this child uncovered the essence of what we ask as we review our life choices: What songs have we stopped singing? What parts of ourselves have we cut off to survive? By requesting a song, this girl prompted not only a performance but also a memory, a dream, and a chance for the executive to bring her entire, authentic self before a stunned audience (who, I suspect, had no idea she had once seen herself on a different stage).

We long for leaders who project a clear and grounded human presence, a fully assembled package with no parts missing—leaders we can copy and admire, whose agendas don't shift like wind socks. We trust people who are transparent—who say what they mean and mean what they say, and whose behaviors align with their belief systems.

Unfortunately, they're not the norm. Both genders leave a little of themselves at the office door when they choose to lead. Men, for instance, must often "get with the program" and conform to the expectations of male leaders. The difference is, men conform to other men and, in that conformity, retain the essence of being a man. Women, on the other hand, often find they must lose qualities associated with being female to blend in with the boys. Once gone, it is terribly difficult to reestablish this voice.

That is why, in an interview at the 2002 White House Project National Women's Leadership Summit, Gloria Steinem gave this message about leadership to young women: "Hang on to your authenticity. Listen to other people, but listen to that inner wisdom most of all." Likewise, in a recent book about the U.S. women senators, *Nine and Counting,* Senator Patty Murray (D-WA) said of public life, "I don't want to lose . . . who I am."

Grasping hard and holding firm to ourselves is much easier when we're surrounded by others like us. Social psychologist Alice Eagly of Northwestern University writes extensively on women, power, and leadership, and she points out that the very rarity of females in high positions has made powerful women disconcerting to both genders. Eagly speaks of a fundamental incongruity between the social roles of "women" (gendered feminine) and of "leader" (gendered masculine). Thus, when women try to be leaders or to be in power, they seem like they are trying to be like men. Many of the first women leaders had to prove themselves "more man than the men" in order to be accepted as strong leaders.

As women expand the definitions of authority, ambition, and ability, they begin to bridge the disconnect between "leader" and "woman." As we rewrite the rules, we begin to change perceptions. We can stop mimicking men as a pathway to authority. We can gain strength from our ambition as we offer every bit of our natural and learned abilities. We can finally be valued for the original we are, rather than the man we sometimes try to be.

During the question-and-answer session that followed my presentation at a 2003 summer session of the Women's Campaign School at Yale University, a bold young African American woman spoke angrily of advice she'd received to appear to be something she wasn't in order to inspire confidence. "Isn't this what we fought for?" she asked, "to be able to be who we are?" A group of top young leaders at Harvard echoed a similar theme when talking to the White House Project about why young women weren't going into politics: They didn't want to compromise their beliefs and strike a balance to be accepted. Young women in business hold similar reservations. In a 2002 *Fast Company* article, one said, "I want a whole and healthy life—and even a recession isn't going to scare me into accepting [a job] that isn't me."

This disconnect can also be true of men, who often cannot bring their caring side to leadership because it would put their masculinity into question. "Traditional standards of masculinity ask people to live horrible lives," says *Newsweek* columnist Anna Quindlen.

"You're never supposed to listen to your heart, only your head. And once you've made a decision with your head, you are never allowed to look back and say, 'Maybe we'd better take a second look at that one.' You're supposed to do all this within a framework of not having time to touch base with what for many of us is the great solace of our existence, our family life."

Disconnects like this can get people killed. Robert McNamara, secretary of defense from 1961 to 1968, during the Vietnam War, explained it this way in 1997 to a *New York Times* reporter, "I try to separate human emotion from the larger issue of human welfare. I try not to let my human emotions interfere with efforts to resolve conflicts." Actress and activist Jane Fonda referred to this quote in a 2003 speech, saying, "This takes my breath away. How can you develop the understanding needed to solve human conflicts if you keep human emotion out of it? Yet this bifurcation between head and heart has characterized most of our leaders for at least as long as I have lived." Or, as a friend of mine who works on artificial intelligence says, "Logic is how we rationalize decisions we have made emotionally."

In the face of so much pressure, how do we help our leaders keep every corner of their psyche? I asked this of a woman who never lost her originality, an American treasure who is consistently named when I ask for examples of authenticity in action—former Texas governor Ann Richards:

"I never pretend to be something I'm not . . . It requires a certain security in who you are. People who try to be something else rather than who or what they are, as you know, usually fall short. They are detected . . . One of the things I find is discouraging about cosmetic surgery is all of us would like to look better, but in doing so we are also saying, 'How I look is insufficient.' It's more evidence of our insecurity, and that insecurity leads to inauthentic and 'pretend' behavior."

Richards confirmed my strong feeling that patterns begin (and can end) young: "I had a father who was tremendously encouraging to me as a child. He made me feel like I was the best, smartest, cutest girl in the world." She described a recent dinner party where a number of accomplished women—heads of corporations, publishers, editors, network executives—were telling their childhood stories. The vast majority said "their fathers had given them encouragement and support as young women."

Richards's mother, on the other hand, was like my own, teaching her how to conform to traditional standards of female behavior because "you don't have as many problems." But again, like my own mother, she taught the young Ann that hard work is "the most important thing in your life . . . I was a risk taker and, in reality, risk taking is not seen as a feminine attribute . . . Safety and protection are the fundamental messages we are given from the time that we are very young: Don't fall down and hurt yourself, don't laugh out loud. All of those behaviors result in little girls not taking risks. Somehow I escaped that."

She also credited her father's sense of humor. "He used to tell these really bawdy dirty jokes and he encouraged that in me . . . I horrified my mother a lot of times and probably embarrassed her. But I was not a good girl, and I am not one now."

Ann Richards was fortunate in her parents, particularly her father, who, as a male, made it especially safe for her to be a different kind of female. By telling her that she needn't be a good girl, he assured she would be a great woman.

The Cutoff

The last girl had barely left the workplace on that first Take Our Daughters to Work Day when the cry went up: "What about the boys!" The Ms. Foundation for Women had not only found a way for adults to help girls keep their feisty, full-voiced selves, we had also invented the first "girl" thing that boys ever wanted to do. Our initial reaction to this wail for equal opportunity was anger. Couldn't girls have *one* lousy day each year, since boys get the other 364? D.C. representative Eleanor Holmes Norton put it best: "Saying we need a Take Our Sons to Work Day is like saying we need a White History Month."

Still, we brought together several national and local organizations that work with boys to get some help and guidance. We felt that any event for boys should closely parallel the girls', giving their brothers a unique experience in the other direction—perhaps visiting a day-care facility or working at a community center. In a fit of idiotic optimism, we even suggested Take Our Sons Home Day, so boys could understand, appreciate, and later participate in that work.

You'd think we'd asked boys to wear frilly dresses. "That would *punish* our sons," came the quick reply from men—a real eye-opener for those of us who had spent decades being "punished." So what *did* they want? Answer: a guarantee that boys would gain and maintain a privileged position in the public world, and that whatever program emerged to ensure that goal would be organized and run by women. In effect, they wanted to perpetuate the patriarchy. I don't know why we were so surprised.

The worst part was knowing these men were not just assuring a smooth power transfer to their gender heirs, along with the expected female support. By not valuing the work of women inside the home, and actually wanting to distance their sons from it, they were reenacting the painful cutoffs boys are asked to make almost from infancy. As Harvard developmental psychologist Elizabeth Debold says, "Because most caretakers are female, it creates a different experience for girls versus boys. When boys start to ask, 'What is it that I am,' they usually answer, 'I'm not Mom, I'm different from Mom, but Mom is my key to survival, where my heart is, the person who has protected me and kept me safe.'" These boys are adamantly told they're not supposed to be anything like their mothers, who at this point is the most important person in their lives. Because this lesson comes at an age when boys are too young to understand it or to fight it, the cutoff becomes particularly painful and confusing.

I remember my grandfather's fury when my toddler son put his head in my lap or clung to me when he was scared. "He's a mama's boy, a sissy," he said in a threatening voice. And he wasn't the only one. Women and men formed a chorus of concern, warning both of us that our connection was unnatural. My son was expected to jerk away, and I was expected to help him.

As Dr. Debold says, in their confusion and pain boys often decide they've got to be invincible. "That's where all-powerful Superman comes in. He left his planet as an infant—sent out into the big wide universe—and he has superpowers unless something from home comes near him. Then he becomes really weak." A perfect metaphor. It takes a superhero to survive the psychological sacrifice boys are asked to make.

For girls, it's different. We've learned through Carol Gilligan's groundbreaking Harvard Project on Women's Psychology and Girls' Development that they cut off older, at adolescence, when they bump into women's power shortage in the world. That's also when many girls begin their quest for perfection as a way to gain acceptance from authority figures, and ultimately from the men they will love. They look to boys and masculine values for validation, rather than trusting what they know to be true.

Their only edge is the age at which they cut off; at least they're old enough to understand what's happening, even if they can't stop it. An added bonus: Girls gain the inner strength that comes with keeping a connection to their mothers, the person who has cared for them and with whom they share gender.

In the end, sadly, we force our children to hack off emotional limbs. Our girls lose agency, voice, anger, and their authentic take on the world—all of which boys get to keep and expand. Boys, however, are asked to jettison their caring sides, their softer emotions, even before they enter kindergarten. Girls keep their relational sensitivity, but it marginalizes them. It's no wonder that both sexes become a perversion of their original intent, closeting the daring of girls and the sensitivity of boys.

The Price We Pay for Manliness

What does it mean to be a man? Michael S. Kimmel, author and expert on masculinity, always asks this question in his nationwide workshops. These are the words and phrases that have remained constant:

> Pressure
> Strong
> Independent
> Bully
> Don't be a girl
> Sex
> Confident
> Denial of feelings
> Don't cry
> Silent
> Do it
> Power
> Don't ask

That last descriptor certainly explains men's almost pathological avoidance of asking for directions when they're lost. The scariest among them: Don't be a girl. About a decade ago, the Michigan Board of Education published a statewide study of students' perceptions of what it means to be male or female. When asked how their lives would be different if they were the opposite sex, nearly 50 percent of the girls spoke of advantages to being a boy, while only 7 percent of the boys saw advantages to being a girl. Although the girls found it interesting or exciting to think of life as a boy, nearly 20 percent of the boys gave extremely hostile, derogatory responses. An alarming number of boys said that they would commit suicide if they suddenly awoke to find they were girls. One boy wrote, "I would *kill* myself *right away* by starting myself on fire so no one knew." Few boys realize they are not so different from the sex they never want to be.

"Boys and girls are not opposite sexes, but neighboring, all from Earth, not Mars and Venus; all psychological studies suggest small differences but, as we say, the between-group variants are not as great as the within-group variants," says Kimmel. The continued pitting of boys against girls, and the "boy crisis" (articles bemoaning how boys are said to be falling behind in education, for instance) misses a real crisis identified by Kimmel: "Violence of a particular kind: bullying, harassment, male-to-male harassment, the environment in which fears of appearing unmanly/sissy are so powerful . . . with the popular put down 'That's so gay.'" As the rapper Eminem tells it: "The lowest thing you can say to a man is to call him a faggot, sissy, punk, take away his manhood. Faggot doesn't mean gay, it means taking away his manhood."

Just as "mean girls" are patrolling the feminine, boys patrol the masculine, and the results are much meaner for all of us. Kimmel obtained the FBI files for all twenty-eight of the school shootings since 1992. This is what he found: "All 28 cases were boys, and 27 . . .

were white boys in rural/suburban schools. . . . All of these 28 boys were beaten up, gay baited, bullied. They were targets. Half were honors students. Some were too fat, too skinny, too big, too small, played in the school band, not athletic; half wore glasses; one started a Greek club at school, one started a philosophy club, both got beaten up for it." According to Kimmel, this happens daily in every school in our country.

Of the twenty-eight cases, only a few were classified as mentally ill. Mostly, they were pushed over the edge by daily harassment and a base disrespect for who they were, until they finally exploded. As Luke Woodham said after he stabbed his mother and killed two students in his Pearl, Mississippi, high school in 1997, "I am not insane, I am angry. I killed because people like me are mistreated every day. I did this to show society, 'Push us and we will push back.'" Kimmel tells the story of a young man in Kentucky who tried to impress his tormentors by showing them his father's gun collection. When it didn't work, he took a host of weapons to school and opened fire, killing three classmates.

In the film *Manufacturing Consent,* a 1993 documentary portrait of linguist, intellectual, and political activist Noam Chomsky, he is asked why he has consistently defended unpopular causes. "When I was in second grade, there was a big fat kid who the bullies all picked on. One day they told him to go outside and wait for them. I walked out and said he shouldn't be alone, and I went and stood with him. The bullies came, and I was ashamed and left. I vowed never again to abandon the underdog." Kimmel uses this story to illustrate why men are "afraid to do the right thing: we're afraid of what other men will do to us" as they work hard to keep their brethren in line.

None of this bodes well for how men learn to lead. A March 2003 article in the *New York Times* describes Secretary of Defense Donald Rumsfeld's grating style as alienating even senior military leaders, who you'd think would welcome a manly slap. Rumsfeld, who was a wrestler at Princeton, is known for a manner that is "equal parts debating club and wrestling match . . . 'He's aggressive, and if you're not aggressive right back, he'll roll right over you,' said one senior officer. . . . 'He takes a strong position for people to shoot at,' " says another. And although he apparently enjoys a debate, the article points out that those who challenge him "must be prepared for withering cross-examination in a style that some . . . find so abrasive that one senior officer has dubbed it 'the wire brush treatment.' "

It's hard to imagine such behavior was hardwired into the arrogant Rummy rather than absorbed through years of studying bad examples of what it means to be a man. Rumsfeld's way of keeping people off guard, not atypical of male leadership, is contrary to successful management pedagogy, to say the least. It's really just high school bullying in high office.

Instead of looking for ways to ensure our sons and daughters are not forced into losing their essence, we keep score on who's ahead—boys or girls. The popular media speak endlessly of a new gender gap where girls are outflanking their brothers in school and entering college in greater numbers. Few of these articles tell why. According to a 2003 piece in *BusinessWeek,* it's pressure born of inequality. Families and schools push girls to get a college degree because they know they'll need to be better prepared just to stay equal. (Even then, it doesn't quite work; a man with a college degree earns $77,963 on average while a woman earns $47,224.)

The same article points to a surefire way to improve boys' school performance: Pay attention to their early emotional lives. A longitudinal study shows that "boys who attend kindergartens that focus on social and emotional skills—as opposed to only academic learning—perform better, across the board, by the time they reach junior high."

Were these skills valued—and they're not because they are mainly associated with females—both genders would be elevated to greater achievement.

A New Kind of Hero

The twists required of "real men" and "real women" make us caricatures of our genders. What's fascinating is that when we see a man who has kept even a slice of his caring side, we find him irresistible. If only we could actually elect a president like the ones in prime time on *The West Wing* and *24*. In our lives and travels we have all found men like them, secure enough in their masculinity to open that door. Slowly they are transforming what it means to be a man.

But slowly is not nearly fast enough in our "boy" institutions, where "girl" qualities are massively undervalued, even though they're exactly what we need. Despite decades of substantial evidence that all organizations benefit from the leadership attributes that women commonly bring, women must often struggle with the cultural paradox of packing the right stuff yet being the wrong sex to unpack it and put it to work.

Women's style of leading has been hailed quietly for years. Leadership theorists like Thomas J. Peters in the 1980s told us we should "pay attention to the employees." In 1990, Peter M. Senge said we should create "learning organizations." Jim Collins explained in 2001 how organizations that go from "good to great" have unassuming leaders with ambition for their institutions. These strengths can be possessed by either gender, but they are broadly associated with women.

Traditionally, our culture sees leadership as men's work; when it is executed by women (or nontraditionally by men), it is often not acknowledged as leadership at all. Although we may wish to think about the organizational dynamics of purpose, effectiveness, and communication as gender free, it's simply not true in most workplaces, and it causes both sexes to assume the "proper" characteristics to fit in.

Academics and private sector consultants have suggested repeatedly that organizations should shift toward less rigid hierarchies, focusing instead on individual learning and overall collaboration. In this way, all workers up and down the food chain would gain a stake in the success of the enterprise. In commerce, this shift equates to healthier business environments and greater profitability. In politics, it brings us closer to democracy.

Sound good? Don't get too excited. These changes—and women's relationship to them—are moving at a crawl. The problem: They are stubbornly diluted by cultural gender schemas. When sound leadership ideas, no matter whose and no matter how exhaustively researched or broadly supported, are essentially seen as expressing feminine behavior, these ideas tend to "disappear."

We need to move far, far away from our current value of "heroic" leadership—where one person is seen as the source of all change and good, leaving everyone else's contribution largely invisible. We need what Joyce K. Fletcher of Simmons College terms "post heroic" leadership, whose mission is relational and collaborative (read female).

Heroic leadership feels more comfortable, of course, because it mimics what we ask of boys in our society—to go it alone bravely (even if they actually don't). It is characterized by a typical male command-and-control style: Orders are given by the leader and carried out by the subordinates. This whole notion of one heroic leader is built on the false assumption (never true, but even more of a lie in today's global environment) that different lines of business are not interdependent, that they operate best in their own silos.

When I discussed Dr. Fletcher's work recently with Barbara Yastine, chief financial officer of Credit Suisse First Boston, she confirmed it: "Companies have to be oriented around the client. Technology makes the world spin faster and, increasingly, people can't operate in silos . . . You have to step back and learn every day. It lends itself to female strengths."

It is clear that we need the "female advantage"—women's ability to communicate across lines of authority, sharing information in a team-spirited work ethic that assumes one person's effectiveness is both dependent on the rest and a contribution to overall excellence. The problem is, many of the behaviors involved in serving clients are not really seen as strengths, but rather as "what women do." It doesn't accrue as leadership—it is simply *expected* as a female gimme. Marriages function this way on a smaller scale, with a relational partner (often the woman) not getting "work credit" for all she does around family and community.

For her book *Disappearing Acts,* Dr. Fletcher studied a group of female design engineers who led through typical female strengths— helping, listening, and teaching—only to find they were viewed as "mothers," not leaders. Why? Because they mended fences with coworkers to maintain relationships, encouraged colleagues and staff, and generally made the group run smoother. As they described it, these tasks were just "what needed to be done," even if they weren't part of a job description. Actions such as these are seldom considered "work," no matter where they are performed—life partners and business executives don't stop to think that they take time and energy, and they're not as easy as a spreadsheet. Again, because this work is not valued, it commonly "disappears."

Behind-the-scenes labor keeps homes running, and it keeps business and government functional. Anyone in an office knows that much of leadership happens out of view, with many players toiling at all levels. But the product is still culturally presented as the work of an individual—a CEO or president of the United States. This basic untruth, embraced wholeheartedly by society because we love a hero, puts glory and blame on one set of shoulders. No one in this process can be entirely himself or herself, including the boss. It's not just our attachment to the hero concept that keeps us from implementing a new kind of leadership, it's also our failure to acknowledge the "gendered" and "disempowered" aspects of the change we need. We talk a good game about participatory leadership, but we rarely act on it in a way that is transformational.

Additionally, women are accustomed to doing whatever it takes to get the job done, often failing to ask for the things they need in order to be effective. An executive coach recently told me: "Give a man a task and he'll say, 'Here's what I need: a team, a budget, financing.' If a woman says, 'Here's what I need,' she looks weak." Women are expected to work with what they have and get the job done, no excuses.

If we could only become Dr. Fletcher's post heroic leaders, who disembody their heroism and model interdependency as the greater "self." This requires more than astute management sense; it requires a willingness to challenge deeply rooted cultural habits that restrict our potential. It requires both genders to bring all of themselves unashamedly to the table, and it demands that we all make it safe and worthy for others to do so.

When I talk to executives about post heroism in current leadership, all roads seem to lead to Ann Moore of Time Inc. One of her first acts in her new job as chair and CEO was to ask all employees to clean out their work closets. Books and stuffed animals and evening bags and even feather boas made their way to the cafeteria, where they were sold for charity. This was not a simple matter of orderliness and philanthropy. Moore was announcing, in a fun sort of way, that she would be cleaning out the closets of old leadership, doing things differently. And she did it in her characteristic participatory style, bringing her staff together in a giant internal garage sale. The *New York Times* missed the point, comparing her to Hazel, a television maid of the 1960s.

We must explore and implement leadership models like Moore's because they are what works best. There is risk: We end up operating *between* existing gender behaviors, yet we are seen *through* the embedded behavioral codes of male/female. The results, in terms of new leadership development, can be thoroughly jinxed. Post heroic men tend to look feminized, the kiss of death to our cultural expectation of them. Post heroic women appear to be doing mothers' work, that is, thinking of others, nurturing relationships, unable to negotiate the toughness of the real (masculine) world. Women who clearly demonstrate a handle on the real world are doubly jinxed as shrews and posers who inadequately respect ancient gender expectations. As a result, no one who practices post heroic leadership is seen as real leader material, even though they are the most real of all.

Gender and Party Politics

Just as our unwavering notions of gender compromise the authenticity of corporations and all who function in them, they also compromise democracy itself as each party becomes locked in a masculine or feminine perspective.

In a 1996 *Atlantic Monthly* article, "Gap Politics," National Public Radio's pop culture commentator Steven D. Stark discusses a historic metaphor for the price paid for rigid ideas of masculinity. "In 1840 the supporters of William Henry Harrison, a war hero, began an American tradition by attacking the incumbent Martin Van Buren as a fop. 'Little Van—the used-up man' his enemies called him, noting that Van Buren favored ruffled shirts and had achieved a new level of effeminacy because he enjoyed taking baths. A victim of his own propaganda, the 68-year-old Harrison refused to wear a coat to his chilly inauguration in March, caught pneumonia, and died a manly death a month later."

When the first Madam President is inevitably elected, she will probably cave to tradition and leave her coat behind, lest she be considered the weaker sex (if she wanted to be the smarter sex, she would move the ceremony to June). But you never know; we should always be prepared for the unexpected. Even the so-called gender gap, one bit of politics tied to women and commonly said to favor Democrats, isn't really female or Democratic. In truth, more men are voting Republican, abandoning the Democratic party (seen as "female" because of its focus on issues like education and child care) in favor of the masculine Republican Party, which has successfully aligned itself with military might, national security, and fiscal management, true or not.

So now we have mommy and daddy parties, separated by the gender of their issues, though even that analysis is not so clean. As Stark says, "In a politics defined by gender identification men are more likely to rally to a male standard than women to a female one." Women will stick loyally to a party even if it doesn't necessarily align itself with traditionally female issues, while the guys abandon the side they perceive as "feminized."

God forbid. A 2003 column in the *New York Times* by Maureen Dowd, discussing evidence that the male Y chromosome is shrinking, inspired this letter to the editor: "There are still plenty of us regular guys who like to drive trucks and eat steak. We're not going away." And, "After eight years of a feminized presidency, most of our society welcomes the resurgence of regular guys who carry on in our battles against terrorists."

You can see why Democrats are having a gender identity crisis. As Democratic pollster Celinda Lake said in Stark's article, "The Republican leaders, who are men, understand the male vote, but I sense that a lot of Democratic male leaders are uncomfortable with their new base of women." Stark agrees that this may be the reason the "Democratic Party is having trouble finding its voice in this new era . . ." I called Lake to see how she felt this gender identification is playing itself out now, seven years later. "Democratic male voters are over the discomfort of being rejected by their peers. But we do have debates in our party about whether we should get more white men."

But Lake still sees the effects of the female base in the party's "tremendous problem with war and homeland security issues. Democrats really are finding it difficult to define a tough alternative, partly because we are fifty polling points behind on 'keeping America strong,' forty-seven points behind on 'the military,' and forty points behind on 'homeland security.' We can't seem to find our voice for the critique.

"I just gave a lecture to male and female interns [on Capitol Hill], but it was the women in the group [they were all Democrats working for Senator Blanche Lincoln of Arkansas] who were raising the issue of how we could possibly have a woman president because foreign leaders would not deal with her. I said, 'How about Madeleine Albright?' And these were the Democratic interns of a woman senator."

In his article Steven D. Stark also talks to Paula M. Baker, associate professor of history at University of Pittsburgh, who saw "general disenchantment with the Democratic Party—and, indeed, with politics and government altogether—as a direct result of sex-based shifts. 'There's a trend in American history that when women enter a particular activity or profession, men then often think less of that domain,' Baker says. 'When anything becomes feminized, the pay diminishes, the stratification in the work increases, and the status diminishes.'" Which is why we *must* start to value female-associated traits.

With storm clouds overhead, the Democratic Leadership Council, centrist arm of the party, gathered in July 2003 to discuss the future. Pollster Mark Penn has found that only 22 percent of white men now identify themselves as Democrats, and the younger they were, the less they did. The DLC warned that unless Democrats become more centrist (read war embracing) and close the gap with the Republicans on national security, they will lose. They criticized the more liberal Howard Dean of Vermont, whose antiwar campaign stance fueled his rise in the polls, and they called for a "concerted effort to appeal to white voters, particularly men and married women."

By this analysis, one could argue that the Democratic Party, with a heavily female base, has lost luster, even on the inside. However, the Democrats are now led by a woman in the House: Nancy Pelosi of California. Will her influence help the party to speak powerfully as itself, in all its female-aligned glory, or will it balk, fearing identification with the less powerful gender? After all, Pelosi is only one woman, which is precisely why we need more women in leadership. Or will Pelosi feel pressured to shift Democrats toward the "party of national security" rather than the "party of Social Security?" Perhaps she should recommend they read up on the need for "human security." If Democrats listen to the concerns of the people about health care, retirement, and other traditional "female" issues, they will see that harnessing their genuine voice, rather than running from it, will make them the real winners.

The Circles of Work and Life

Our bifurcated world of public and private life, of men's work and women's work, of men's issues and women's issues, offers few options for either gender. It would help if we stopped thinking of public and private as completely separate spheres, but rather as two overlapping circles that often intersect in that place called community. The trick will be moving those circles into ever greater overlap until we finally create a new way to lead.

Women are more and more dissatisfied with organizations that fail to fully value their work, or to see them as leaders. Contrary to popular belief, women don't always point to work and family conflicts as the main reason for leaving their jobs. Rather, they are tired of challenging the inefficiencies and ineffectiveness of the workplace—they want to work *differently.* So they stop out, drop out, create companies, take lower level jobs, become consultants. And our workplaces lose the very transformational leadership that we need, and possibly (as a top male CEO recently confided to me) the most talented women we have.

But what if we shift the values of the private sphere more solidly into the public one? We might find ourselves creating teams and not just depending on individuals, treasuring family life and not just work, showing empathy and not just enforcing rules. "Good to great" executives say they have balanced lives, and they talk of loving their jobs and their colleagues. Silos are dead; the isolation of our former life has gone the way of the dinosaur, replaced by technology and cultural awareness across global boundaries. We are now forced to understand how the rest of the world works and thinks.

Often when change of such magnitude peeks from under the security blanket of patterns, we experience backlash. The suffragists and abolitionists saw it when they worked toward a fundamental alteration in an unfair system. However, my proposal isn't so much about role *change,* to borrow a term from feminist scholars Joyce Gelb and Marian Lief Palley. It's about what I will call role *expansion.* Women who enter the public sphere don't just leave the private behind; they take it with them. If we put more women in the public realm, men might feel they can bring more of their private sides into the workplace. Public and private, male and female, then join to become community.

The rub is, if women aren't focusing their energies almost entirely on the private sphere, as they traditionally have, and are instead bringing their values to the public sphere, who's going to do that private work? Will whole families and communities fall apart? Will men have to be full-time soccer dads? That's not the real problem, though it is the biggest societal worry.

The real problem is that the public realm as it exists today simply doesn't work. Without the voices of women it is impoverished in every sphere, and that's a crisis. Women's leadership, with its focus on community, could neutralize the nastier aspects of capitalism and shift the balance of our democracy, making it about *all* the people, using *all* the resources we have to make "work" a community value. Everyone can be tough and caring, everyone can be a parent, everyone can speak as an individual, not as an inauthentic imitator based on twisted gender roles. We need those public and private circles of influence to almost fully overlap.

It's not hard to do. Those circles move closer every time we keep our values, in spite of the cultural norm. It happens each time we encourage men to stay home with children, and women to run a company. It happens when we let boys cry and we let girls play sports. They move closer when we hear a woman say she wants it all, and we ask her what we can do to help her get it. It happens with every new child-care program at work, with fully supported paternity leave, with communication and understanding from the top down. It happens when we tell our daughters they look just fine, and urge our sons to deliver that message to their girlfriends. Each small step brings us closer to the collective nature of community leadership. When we finally assign value to the assets of women, when we encourage men to lead relationally, when we merge our public and private selves to create strong bonds at work and at home, we will alter the meaning of leadership.

7

CULTURE

You can't be what you can't see.

—Marian Wright Edelman,
founder and president,
The Children's Defense League

Chief Wilma Mankiller once exhorted me to "go where the people are." So I voted for President Barbie. I'm not sure that's what Wilma had in mind, but Barbie linked the past (my daughters loved theirs), the present (my granddaughter must have dozens of them), and the future (if girls are going to play with Barbie anyway, we might as well give her some power). President Barbie connected pop culture, media, politics, and business as only an icon can.

Soon after we began the White House Project in 1998, a young woman in the office of Barbara Lee, one of the founders of the project, suggested we create President Barbie to coincide with the 2000 presidential election. I was horrified. Hadn't I just spent the last decade dealing with unrealistic body messages to girls, including those sent by the rail-thin, high-heeled Barbie? Who cares if she's practically part of my own family? Who cares if Girls Inc., a respected group dedicated to empowering girls, had sponsored Working Woman Barbie? She was a nonstarter on our team.

It wasn't until I visited Mattel to raise money for our struggling project that I spontaneously blurted, "Why don't you make a President Barbie and turn that dream house into a White House, so she'll have something to dream about?" They were interested, and suddenly I was negotiating terms: We would partner with Girls Inc. on the accompanying educational materials. There would be a girls' bill of rights and, on the box, a sample inaugural address. Mattel would also create a Web site telling girls about the presidency and how to run for it.

We asked Jill Barad, then president of Mattel, to make black, white, Latina, and Asian dolls. She said yes. We asked that Barbie stand on her own (instead of being propped up by a stand). She said she couldn't. We asked for a White House. She was completely intrigued and said she would make at least a few. (She left Mattel soon after, so there was no White House and, to our dismay, no Asian dolls either.)

As befitting a commander in chief, President Barbie got quite a bit of visibility in the press. She made President Bill Clinton's White House press briefing, where Press Secretary Joe Lockhart had to give odds on Malibu Barbie's impact on the presidential campaign. She made the daily television talk shows and scores of magazines. She was fought over at both political conventions (we didn't have enough to give away). President Barbie did what she was meant to do: She hijacked a cultural symbol and started a conversation. Her presence made both big and little girls ask a new question during the 2000 presidential elections: Where are the women?

My friend Kathleen Hall Jamieson—who was always supportive of the fledgling White House Project's goal of changing the culture, creating a climate where many women could assume leadership roles— made the best use of President Barbie. After overcoming her misgivings, she dutifully gave one to her niece, whose mother put it in a closet until history caught up with culture. Jamieson made her get the doll down, and take out Ken and the other Barbies too. Once she had a quorum, they played, "Let's call a joint session of Congress."

Culture as Change Agent

Poet Audre Lorde said, "The master's tools will never dismantle the master's house." However, when it comes to culture and women's roles in our society, that's exactly what can be done. Television, movies, journalism, advertising, toys, and books present a huge opportunity to stretch the collective imagination, showing women and men in nontraditional roles and changing the perception of what is possible in the real world.

Take Our Daughters to Work taught me once and for all about the power of culture to make change. Prior to TODTW a decade ago, my colleagues and I spent two years trying unsuccessfully to get media attention for research about girls' declining self-esteem at adolescence. We traveled, we spoke, we distributed Carol Gilligan's scholarly work, we conducted our own studies, we gave briefings to empty rooms, we tried to organize local and national women's groups on the issue. No takers.

Why, then, after all this effort, was Take Our Daughters to Work the successful vehicle for the message? Because it gave people one small thing they could do to make a difference in their daughters' lives. Still, it might have stayed an obscure effort had the media not propelled it to fame. Newspapers, magazines, television, and radio spread the word about how to participate, then they documented the girls in action.

As of 2003, a third of all Americans had participated in the program, changing future options for millions of girls and placing the day in the middle of popular culture, where we learn about and create trends. The images we present in culture transform who we are, what we might become, and what we think. The government does it almost daily by managing the news through scores of handlers. Carla Santos Shamberg of Jersey Films, who discovered and then co-produced *Erin Brockovich,* reminded me recently of one of the more pointed examples: the Bureau of Motion Pictures of the early 1940s, which helped Hollywood shape public perceptions of World War II.

The bureau issued *The Government Information Manual for the Motion Picture* as a prompt for filmmakers to ask themselves, "Will this picture help to win the war?" It also read scripts, and it requested images of "people making small sacrifices for victory—making them voluntarily, cheerfully, and because of the people's own sense of responsibility." Shamberg says, "This overall censorship of the media had a profound effect on the way Americans lived and what they believed."

No one works harder at (or has a better grasp of) this manipulation than advertisers. That's what they do for a living; they have built a $236.9 billion industry to collect data on our buying habits, then convince us to change them. They know that women represent 83 percent of the purchasing power in America, an astonishing $3 trillion market. Another of their potent weapons: pitching to young people.

In her new book, *Branded: The Buying and Selling of Teenagers,* Alissa Quart brings the phenomenon up to date in an era where kids are bombarded by information. She says, "Teen-oriented brands now aim to register so strongly in kids' minds that the appeal will remain for life." As a 2003 *New York Times* article on the book points out, "Companies rush to create emotional relationships with [teenagers] centered on idealized notions of how their bodies should look and what they should buy. Brands, in [the author's] view, be-

come surrogate parents." Kids can't even escape it at school: Pepsi
and Coke have contracts in 150 school districts across twenty-nine
states, and snacks like Oreo cookies get mentioned in textbooks.

Some commercials openly sell values as well as products. Mastercard is a premier example, with its amazing "priceless" ads on television. In one version, a father takes his kids to a professional baseball
game; we learn the prices of the tickets, the hot dogs, the souvenirs.
We also learn that the opportunity to take our kids to their first game
is "priceless" ("but for everything else, there's Mastercard"). Each ad
plays to connection through family and community. It will come as
no surprise that the ad that launched the campaign was created at
McCann-Erickson by a woman.

Political candidates also infiltrate the culture through media, and
they did it with 1.2 million ads at a cost of $771 million during the
2000 presidential election. In *Politics, Media, and Modern Democracy,*
published in 1996, authors Paolo Mancini and David L. Swanson
say, "It is through television that the attachments are formed that
link citizens to their representatives. Thus, skillful use of television to
cultivate personal support is regarded as essential to political success
in every democracy. . . ." (Howard Dean has pioneered the use of a
newer medium, the Internet, to build a national fund-raising network
for his 2004 presidential run.) Culture can also move in the opposite
direction, building a political career from a celebrity base. The 1980
election of Ronald Reagan, who started his career as a B-movie actor, is the most obvious example. There's also Jesse Ventura, former
professional wrestler who became governor of Minnesota in 1998.
The 2003 California recall election was filled with names from popular culture, and the winner for governor: none other than the "the
terminator" himself, Arnold Schwarzenegger.

Think back to the hundreds of icons of the past decades and the
influence they've had on the way we dress, the music we buy, the
books we read, the way we think: Madonna's bald sexuality, the Bea-

tles' haircuts, Twiggy and the miniskirt, rappers and the baggy fashion of teenage boys, Jackie Kennedy's pillbox hats, the romance of 1940s movies that convinced women their lives would be like musicals, Harry Potter and Oprah Winfrey and the culture of reading, the lottery and its ability to convince us we can actually win, the commercial hip-hop culture and its message that women are good for sex and men are good for money. We absorb cultural stimuli, then adapt the messages to our lives. Sometimes they are passing fads. Sometimes they are much more.

In the 2004 edition of the *Unofficial Unbiased Insider's Guide to the 328 Most Interesting Colleges,* published by Kaplan Press, the authors asked school guidance counselors to name the most influential TV shows and movies in terms of nudging students toward a career. In television, the top five were *CSI* (forensics), *ER* (medicine), *Law & Order* (law), *Boston Public* (teaching), and *The Practice* (law). In movies, they were *A Beautiful Mind* (math), *Legally Blonde* (law), *Drumline* (not for careers, but to draw attention to historically black colleges), *The Lord of the Rings* (computer graphics), and tied at fifth were *Mr. Holland's Opus* (education) and *The Sum of All Fears* (CIA).

One organization has been quite deliberate about using culture to influence careers. The Alfred P. Sloan Foundation funds film school awards for screenwriting, film production, and film animation; it partners with film festivals like Sundance; it works directly with TV writers and producers—all in an effort to challenge stereotypes about scientists and engineers.

Advocates for Youth, a nonprofit group that focuses on reproductive and sexual health, created the Media Project to directly educate producers and writers. They met with the producers of *Judging Amy,* and the show did an episode on the debate between abstinence and sex education. They met with a writer from *Law & Order: Special Victims Unit* to help the popular show in its portrayal of transsexuals. The executive producer of *Girlfriends* called Robin Smalley, who runs the Media Project, to ask her to educate the cast on HIV/ AIDS so she could gain their support for a story line. She brought women with AIDS to the set, and the cast was very moved.

Information through storytelling can have a sweeping effect, interrupting national and cultural patterns. A South African soap opera, *Soul City,* broadcast an episode where domestic violence was stopped with the help of common kitchen tools. A violator would be surrounded, and pots and spoons would be banged until the cops arrived to take him away. When this strategy started to be used in real life, domestic violence declined in that country.

Martin Kaplan, associate dean at the Annenberg School for Communication at the University of Southern California, told me of another powerful example of entertainment education: *Simplemente Maria.* This Spanish-language TV series, originating in Peru, tells the story of a young maid who educates herself and marries her literacy tutor. On the day of the "marriage," ten thousand fans converged on the church to watch the filming. Even the military junta is said to change the times of meetings so they can tune in. *Simplemente Maria* has altered the formula for who wins and loses, empowering women in its wake. It has also taken adult literacy in Peru to extraordinary levels. "*Maria* has become a cultural phenomenon," says Dr. Kaplan. "When she got married in one episode, all of South America shut down to watch."

The Chicken or the Egg

Does culture simply reflect society, or does it change the society it serves, moving it a step beyond its comfort zone? Television provides a mirror on the answer. Even in its infancy, our most powerful and intimate medium gave us both *Ozzie and Harriet,* the perfect American couple, and *I Love Lucy,* an intercultural marriage between an unforgettable redhead and her Cuban bandleader husband (the first show appeared in 1951 and hasn't been off the air since). Lucille Ball and Desi Arnaz will forever remain landmark figures in entertainment, both for their humor and their challenge to taboos. At a time when couples like them were shunned offscreen for showing affection, Lucy and Ricky Ricardo flaunted theirs, playing shamelessly to his Latin accent and showing a pregnant Lucy in a television first. Yes, they were also stereotypes of the public and private (it was the fifties, after all)—Lucy stayed home while Ricky had a career—but the character Lucy wore her ambition on her sleeve, clumsily trying to break into show business. She was also the first woman TV star, making it easier for all women in her wake.

The 1960s took us to other worlds through Gene Roddenberry's *Star Trek,* which began in 1966 when America was trying to put a man on the moon. The show's hour-long fantasies of space travel, and its moralistic story lines, did more than entertain. One of the most memorable shows, first aired in 1969 during the struggle for civil rights, discussed the "race wars" on a planet where part of the population was black on the left side of their bodies and white on the right, and the other half had the opposite coloring. In the episode only two "opposites" are left, one a cop and the other his "criminal" prey because of his coloring, still fighting, even though their planet is long dead from bigotry.

The cast, too, was a model of gender, race, and international (and interplanetary) cooperation, with a black female communications officer, Asian and Russian helmsmen (this during the cold war), and a Vulcan. Captain James T. Kirk of the Federation Starship *Enterprise* was white, of course, but he was also empathetic and principled. The crew, in fact, frequently used transformational behavior, with teamwork and communication across ranks.

In 1966 we were also introduced to TV's first single, independent woman—neither pitied as an old maid nor personally unhappy—when Marlo Thomas starred in *That Girl*. As Thomas tells it, "Being a single woman on television was so unusual that the powers-that-be tried to make my character live at home with her parents. I had to fight tooth and nail for my own apartment."

Thomas's Ann Marie was a "perfect girl," but she opened the door to generations of interesting imperfection: Mary Tyler Moore, an even older unmarried woman; Bea Arthur, a gray-haired curmudgeon; Roseanne Barr, an irreverent "domestic goddess"; Candice Bergen, a single mom attacked by Vice President Dan Quayle for immorality; Ellen DeGeneres, bursting out of the closet; the casts of *Ally McBeal* and *Sex and the City*, taking women's desire and independence right to the limit, if not beyond.

Women now pepper the most watched ensembles in television: *CSI* (both of them) and *Law & Order* (all three of them). There's a leading female doctor on Lifetime in *Strong Medicine*, a James Bond clone in *Alias*, and a press secretary, a national security adviser, and a first lady with an M.D. on *The West Wing*. Scientists, lawyers, detectives, doctors, government leaders, and spies—Lucille Ball would have been proud. But she would have been even prouder if, when the producers of *The West Wing* got rid of the show's original vice president, they had replaced him with a woman.

Clearly, society has progressed in its culture as it watches lifestyle alternatives played out in the comfort of home. Now it is time to push culture even further—making women into *leaders* and not just leading ladies. There is no doubt that we have strong women in equally strong roles, but they are not always in places where society needs to see them: at the top. We did get a female captain on *Star Trek: Voyager*, but she and the crew lived in daily crisis, trying to get home when they are accidentally tossed to the other end of the galaxy. Still, we'll take it.

Why is it that so few women run anything in the fictional world of movies and television? I asked Stacey Snider, Universal Pictures

chair who paid $20 million to get Julia Roberts to play Erin Brock-
ovich, why there aren't more films where women are shown as leaders. Her answer: the box office. Rachel Abramowitz, *Los Angeles
Times* columnist and author of *Is That a Gun in Your Pocket: Women's
Experience of Power in Hollywood,* agrees. Hollywood has become a
global industry; for studios to make money on films, they need to
sell their ancillary rights, which is more easily done with action films
(most of which star men). Abramowitz says that "complex female
characters just don't cut it in the international market, where U.S.
movies must compete to succeed." Frank Rich, columnist at the
New York Times, adds: "These movies must be understood by people
who may not understand America. They're comic books, pitched to
a younger demographic."

Which could be one reason the shelf life of an actress is so short.
Hollywood, after all, has a youth obsession, so there aren't many
roles for older women. Actress Rosanna Arquette, forty-four, made
a documentary about it for Showtime called *Searching for Debra
Winger,* named for the former star who now lives in a suburb of New
York with her husband and children; she felt forced to choose her
family over her career. As actress Sharon Stone says in the film, "I try
to make decisions that also include how it will affect women who
come after me. [Whether it's] fighting for money . . . or fighting for
a kind of a job or fighting for the freedom to be powerful and naked
in a movie and not be cheap or degraded for it."

In a way, the cultural change we need would benefit older actresses—after all, leaders are rarely twenty-five years old. It's a difficult sell, though, and you need powerful help to even start. Carole
Black, president and CEO of Lifetime Television, and Pat Mitchell
of PBS, accompanied the White House Project to Hollywood in
2001, when we pitched a different vision of women to a group of
television screenwriters and producers.

The folks from *CSI* came up to us afterward and said, "We could make the mayor of Las Vegas a woman." We wished we'd thought of it, but it hasn't happened yet. Gene Herd, executive director of the Hollywood Radio and Television Society, was so intrigued that he suggested we make a presentation at one of their meetings, where we could hit hundreds at once with the idea of women leaders on television. A committee formed. Everyone seemed enthusiastic. We didn't hear from them for months, and when we did, they told us that, on second thought, there were already a lot of "leading ladies." This was hardly the point, I told them, since leading ladies aren't usually leaders in the roles they play. They were not moved.

We also tried movies, specifically Miramax's Project Greenlight, the Ben Affleck/Matt Damon competition that seeks submissions from untested screenwriters, the prize being a $1 million contribution to the project's budget from Miramax and a guarantee to release the film. The Miramax folks were generous with advice on how we might start a similar competition for scripts about women leaders. Since Miramax already had Project Greenlight, we went to see Warner Bros.' head of publicity, who offered to see if writers would welcome a contest for these types of scripts. The answer was no.

Here's what I'm convinced it takes: Tom Hanks and Julia Roberts, the cast of *Friends*—big stars, bankable stars, demanding these plot lines. Hanks could say he'd happily play a supporting role for a great script and a great actress. Moneymakers like these are the only voices that Hollywood appears to hear and respect, and they could change the culture almost overnight. Tom Hanks did it with *Philadelphia,* which humanized the AIDS crisis, because he agreed to play a gay man.

With stars on board, we could tackle another problem: the point of creation. Martha M. Lauzen of San Diego State University examined the 2001–2002 prime-time season in her study, *Boxed In.* Among her findings: Men created and wrote about 80 percent of TV dramas and sitcoms in this medium of the writer. "Overall, women comprised 23 percent of all creators, executive producers, producers, directors, writers, editors, and directors of photography last season. This percentage has remained virtually unchanged for the last three seasons. However, the representation of women writers declined dramatically last season, dipping from 27 percent in [the previous year] to 19 percent . . ."

On a 2002 visit to Hollywood, I saw a wonderful screenwriter and TV producer, Diane English, the creator of *Murphy Brown*. I asked her if she would consider writing a script about a woman president. A year later she had a deal with Disney to write and direct a movie on the topic, and I plan to do everything I can to support it. That's how the culture changes.

Case Study: The American Presidency

If we ever have any doubts that starring roles—and the stars themselves—affect our perceptions, we need look no further than the fictional presidency.

Right now two men are playing the president on weekly prime-time shows: Martin Sheen on *The West Wing* and Dennis Haysbert on *24*. As the first African American to play a president in a TV series, Haysbert provides a redefinition of what the "leader of the free world" looks like, and he allows other people of color to see themselves in that role. Haysbert, talking to *Back Stage* magazine in 2003, described how when he testified at a hearing on Hollywood's portrayal of Washington, people from limo drivers to congressional pages, Secret Service agents to guards, called him "Mr. President." The article also points out a commonality among firsts, be they African American or women: the demand for perfection. "[The character] had to be squeaky clean," Haysbert said. "Had to be. They would have found any kind of chink in his armor to exploit." In a fascinating life-imitating-art moment, Haysbert is often asked to run for office. As he says, "It has, first and foremost, seriously put it in people's mind that it is possible."

Many men have had a crack at a silver-screen presidency, including Harrison Ford, Gene Hackman, Morgan Freeman, Jeff Bridges, Michael Douglas, and Chris Rock. One woman also got that chance: Polly Bergen in the 1964 comedy, *Kisses for My President*. Fred MacMurray played her husband, and the focus was on his experience as "first man." In the end, Bergen is overwhelmed by the job and happily resigns when she becomes pregnant.

We're getting closer, though. In 1997, Glenn Close played the tough and capable vice president in *Air Force One*, making life-and-death decisions to save the president. In the 2000 film *The Contender*, Joan Allen starred as a senator who is about to be nominated as vice president. Both Close and Allen played admirable, tough leaders, and they helped to change perceptions of what a vice president looks like. Continuous exposure to images—even fictional ones—takes on the power of truth. That is why we react so strongly when we see damaging stereotypes. That is why, when we witness only men in leadership roles, it becomes our reality, our norm, though we know women are just as ready and capable. Female leaders are simply an unfamiliar sight—an enormous issue if we are to put women in equal power.

Marlo Thomas insists the time is right for Madam President: "It's just a matter of a great script." When I asked screenwriter Raphael Yglesias, who wrote *Fearless* and *Les Misérables*, about women leaders in films, he answered honestly, "The fact that fewer actresses [than actors] are considered capable of 'opening' a picture . . . has a profound impact on how often a writer conceives of a story . . . centered on a female lead." Yglesias sees some light as actresses gain power at the box office, "but there's still a gap and that's a drag on developing stories about women." A friend, he said, once wrote a script commissioned by Faye Dunaway about a woman president "but during the writing [Dunaway] kept insisting he make her character less decisive, shying away from what are, in fact, routine acts of leadership for men." Odd, he pointed out, since the script was under way during the era of former British Prime Minister Margaret Thatcher, a woman who took her nation to war.

Even if Yglesias writes a strong script, and even if Marlo Thomas agrees to champion it, we've still got a deficit. Filmmaking is a director's medium—female directors are more likely to want to tell this type of story but, unfortunately, there aren't many of them. A Hollywood billboard during the 2003 Oscars (sponsored by the Guerrilla Girls, a group of art professionals who patrol discrimination in their world) put it bluntly: EVEN THE U.S. SENATE IS MORE PROGRESSIVE THAN HOLLYWOOD. FEMALE SENATORS: 14%. FEMALE DIRECTORS: 4%.

The Celluloid Ceiling, a 2002 study by Dr. Lauzen, who also did the prime-time research, analyzed the employment of women in the top 250 domestic grossing films of 2002. It provides quite a bleak picture: Only 7 percent of all directors were women, and more than nine out of ten films were directed by men, despite the fact that nearly equal numbers of men and women go to movies.

Just as Dennis Haysbert's black president had to be a perfect character, so, too, women directors have to score an immediate hit. Debra Zimmerman, executive director of Women Make Movies, which distributes films made by women, says, "A man's first film can be a flop but he will always get a second chance, yet the film world is littered with women directors who couldn't get their second films made." Allison Anders, taking a break from directing an episode of *Sex and the City*, says, "I've seen men who can't direct their way out of a paper bag make a film that bombs, and they turn around and get a huge studio film . . . When our movies don't [succeed], we don't get a chance to make a second movie."

Major actresses, however, are helping each time they step to the plate, using their star power to get films made. Twenty years ago, Barbra Streisand led the way as the first woman to produce, direct, and act in the same film, *Yentl*. Penny Marshall made the leap from TV's *Laverne & Shirley* to directing movies, with winners like *A League of Their Own, Big,* and *Awakenings*. There are also high-powered executive producers like Julia Roberts (*Stepmom*), Bette Midler (*Beaches* was her first; most recently her All Girl Productions produced *Divine Secrets of the Ya-Ya Sisterhood*), and Reese Witherspoon (*Legally Blonde 2*). Drew Barrymore produced both films in the *Charlie's Angels* franchise. We've also got a host of recent films (not your typical Hollywood fare) that focus on younger women and their struggles to control their destinies, all but one of which were directed by women:

- *Real Women Have Curves:* A first generation Mexican-American teenager receives a scholarship to Columbia University and battles the tradition that would have her stay home.
- *Bend It Like Beckham:* A talented athlete wants to bend the ball into the net like English soccer star David Beckham, but she must first bend the rules in her Indian family.
- *Rabbit-Proof Fence:* Set in Australia in 1931, when government policy required half-caste children (Aboriginal mothers and white fathers) to be trained as servants, the film follows three young girls who escape from the training facility and, using rabbit-proof fences as their guide, walk fifteen hundred miles home.
- *Whale Rider:* Pai is the surviving grandchild of Koro, chief of a Maori tribe, who is blinded by tradition that only a male heir can lead the

tribe—until he realizes that Pai is the leader he's
been waiting for.

Popular culture is not simply entertainment, to be watched and
discarded; it stays with us long after we digest it, and it provides the
young with opportunities to see themselves in life roles. It tells them
what a CEO looks like and what a cop looks like, what a stay-at-
home parent looks like, what an athlete looks like. And what a president looks like.

Give Us the Ball, Coach

Since the passage in 1972 of Title IX, which guaranteed equal opportunities for men and women in education, we have seen a seismic
shift in the genders we watch on the field and on the court—and
along with it a shift in girls' strength, power, and body image. Think
what sports do for boys in building character and bodies, making
virtue of teamwork and creating heroes. They are now doing the
same for girls. A 2002 OppenheimerFunds survey of female executives found that more than four in five played sports as girls, and that
they felt it contributed to their future success in business.

When my oldest daughter, who is now in her late thirties, was in
her early teens, she was the only girl on an all-male soccer team. She
played for six months before quitting. The boys wanted her gone,
both because she was a girl and because she didn't excel as a begin-
ner at the sport. She was a sterling athlete—champion backstroker
on the swim team, dynamite infielder on her softball team, 1975
holder of the school sit-up record at one hundred (the coach told
her to stop after the last boy dropped out at ninety, but she could
have done more). Yet no one believed in her potential, including the

male soccer coach. Through the years, my daughter has watched from the sidelines as the world of competition evolved into one of acceptance for women in sports and also of team professionalism.

After the U.S. women's soccer team won the World Cup in 1999, they were on late-night television and the cover of every news magazine. The most popular and visible star, Mia Hamm, who has scored more goals in international competition than any man or woman, has had multiple endorsements, including Nike, Gatorade, Kraft Foods, and Mastercard. Team captain Julie Foudy, president of the Women's Sports Foundation, is rumored to be interested in running for office.

Since I didn't grow up playing team sports, I didn't understand its early importance to women and girls. It wasn't until several years ago, when I walked into Madison Square Garden for my first professional women's basketball game, that it hit home: The WNBA (Women's National Basketball Association) had invaded the all-male sanctity of the Garden. Members of the New York Knicks attended. Boys wore shirts with the names of their favorite female players on the back. I watched these prancing women bounce from basket to basket, cracking their heads on the floor and fighting for possession of the ball. They played with passion, and they lost with grace. ESPN and Oxygen broadcast their toughness and persistence, showing national audiences the qualities of champions—and leaders.

We've seen an explosion of women athletes as role models, some so recognizable that we only need refer to them by their first names: Steffi, Mia, Venus, Serena, Nadia, Flo Jo, Annika. When Annika Sorenstam recently became the first woman in almost sixty years to play in a men's Professional Golf Association (PGA) event (the last was Babe Didrikson Zaharias in 1945), every network in America hit the bars to ask guys what they thought. The overwhelming response: Sorenstam's bravery and drive were nothing but good for the game of golf.

Don't Just Watch TV! Do Something!

When Gloria Steinem turned fifty, people tackily and frequently commented on how good she looked for her age. Her response became a legendary T-shirt slogan, THIS IS WHAT 50 LOOKS LIKE. Soon, if we get enough women at the top, we'll be able to say, "This is what leadership looks like."

Getting there takes a degree of activism that most women can't afford, especially if it's only for themselves. So here's what I suggest: Grab a girl—she doesn't have to be your daughter—and devise ways for the two of you to send messages to the decision makers about what you will accept (*Bend It Like Beckham*) and what you won't (the World Wrestling Federation). Hit them in the wallet, with market share and box office haul.

If you see something you like, let those at the top know by supporting it financially. Write them a letter; ask the girl to write too, and you'll double your positive response. When you see something you don't like, do the same. And educate your family. When my kids and I would see a sexist commercial on TV, I'd get their attention through humor: "Hey, look! There's a woman on the hood of that car! We didn't get a woman when we bought our last car!"

In the movie business the statistics that are monitored most closely by the industry are ticket sales in the first weekend after a new release. Pick films you might enjoy that are released by women directors and form a "first weekend club." If you're not sure which films qualify, you can check www.moviesbywomen.com.

Form teams of activism with your girl partner, creating whole networks of your own. Maybe Elle Woods of *Legally Blonde 2* went a little far with her Million Dog March, but it made me laugh, and laughter is among the world's most powerful change agents. Encourage these girls to become a new generation, making different decisions when they invariably have the jobs that kept their mothers a step down. We can't wait for someone else to do it. And neither can they.

As Pat Mitchell of PBS said, "Imagine if half the entertainment companies were run by women . . . would there be a different reality on television? In the movies? . . . Of course there would be. And that's the point."

8

THE BUSINESS OF TRANSFORMATION

To those who question whether women would change the nature of political power, or whether political power would change the nature of women, there can be only one answer—let's try it. Let's find out.

—*Bella Abzug, late Democratic congresswoman, cofounder of Women's Environment and Development Organization*

Fresh eyes and fresh solutions applied to old and abiding problems, unique skills honed through family and community service, the opportunity for a true democracy, transforming business and politics: These are the advantages of the leadership of women. We know that the values women commonly bring to the workplace—empathy and inclusion across lines of authority, relational skills, and community focus—are the tickets to success there. We know that broader societal legislation, benefiting everyone, is more likely to pass if women are elected to office. We know the power of women as peacemakers in a troubled world. And we know the expectations of the next generation—girls expect to lead *and* breed, boys expect to work *and* to play with their kids. It's time for real and permanent power sharing—women, side by side with men, can and must help run the world. But if none of those imperatives work for you, try this one: It's good for business.

● ● ●

Harry Reasoner, a managing partner at the Vinson & Elkins law firm in Houston, showed a PowerPoint presentation at the annual partners retreat in 2001. According to a June 2003 article in *The American Lawyer,* he first flashed a black-and-white picture of "three older white men in business suits," saying they represented the firm's clients "for the first 75 years." Then he showed a colorful image of three smiling women—in-house lawyers from Shell Oil Company. "This is what our clients look like today."

The image of client, the image of leader, the image of woman. Reasoner, with simple elegance, began both the education of his partners and the transformation of his firm. It was not only the right thing to do, it was the *only* thing to do. After all, some clients (including Shell) now wanted to know the percentage of women and minorities who worked on their litigation, even asking for a breakdown on their bills. Others wouldn't hire firms without a solid mixture. Closer to home, Reasoner's daughter had become a lawyer and a mother. The circles of work and family were overlapping.

And that's how change begins—a little bit business, a little bit personal. This same law firm examined its attrition rate in 2000, and found that 88 percent of women leave the firm by their seventh year, as opposed to 63 percent of men, a major reason why they had so few women partners (though, in truth, they just about mirrored the national partner average for women of 16 percent; the national average for women managing partners—the big bosses—is 5 percent). Attorney Marie Yeates, who saw the dangers and prepared Reasoner's slide show, helped found the Women's Career Development Council at the firm that fall.

Vinson & Elkins is a blueprint for how a system alters itself before it becomes extinct. It is a story filled with players who stepped up to the plate: a woman leader who took action, her male ally who wasn't afraid to challenge the system, females who weren't afraid to speak the truth—and business imperatives that guaranteed the outcome.

The women at the firm, when asked about the problems they faced, spoke freely. Yes, there were work and family issues, but there were also career development issues. The women associates, all 150 of them, told board members they were a bit "mystified" by what it took to succeed there. A golf handicap? And what if they wanted to be moms? Would it count against them? Was anyone already on a flexible schedule at the firm? After digging only an inch below the surface, they found that men had similar issues.

The Vinson & Elkins of today is much different from the one that existed when Reasoner made his presentation. Working "mother" lunches have morphed into working "parent" lunches. The firm has defined and rolled out a program of core competencies, and partnership is now based on levels of expertise, assuring that part-timers have a shot at the top. It has revamped practices to assure that flextime is both gender neutral and based on a business case (all who have applied so far have met that standard), and it has begun a mentoring program. The attrition rate for females is now the same as males. In spring 2004, the women associates will meet again with the board, and this time they will have a story of transformation. "Female" values were put front and center, and *everybody* won.

When the culture of one institution starts to change, it can spread like a brushfire. Angela Bradstreet, a partner at the San Francisco law firm of Carroll, Burdick & McDonough, formed an independent blue ribbon group on the West Coast that called itself the No Glass Ceiling Task Force, with members of powerful private and corporate firms signing on. As a result, more than sixty firms (mostly in San Francisco) have initialed a document with concrete objectives that was drafted in 2002:

- 25 percent women partners by the end of 2004
- At least one female chair or managing partner, either firmwide or in a branch office, by 2005
- Retention of men and women attorneys at equal rates by 2004

When these firms reach their goals, I feel certain they will burst more old seams by moving toward flexible schedules, part-time partners, and child care—not because they're good for women, but because they're good for everyone.

Bradstreet is now fielding questions from the bar associations of New York and Texas, and she is helping the women of Germany with a similar initiative. When asked how the firm had done so much in a country highly resistant to quotas, she shot back, "These are business goals. This is good for business. When corporations are saying they're not going to send their business to a law firm unless the law firm signs on to the glass ceiling initiative, it really makes an impact. People really start to listen. It's good for business."

The potential to transform an entire industry now exists because a few law firms noticed that women were good for business. Rhetoric is moving toward reality, and not a moment too soon. In her 1997 book, *Why Work Doesn't Work Anymore: Women, Work, and Identity,* Liz Perle McKenna talks of "a Darwinian system that weeds out those with no stomach for politics, competition or mono-focused ambition." Mainly, women.

In the words of Susan D. Toscani, an executive director at *Forbes* magazine and founder of Catholic Women@Work, it's less about having families than it is about having an identity: "I offer you not only my own testimony, but also that of all the other American working women I've met and with whom I've interacted over the years: Married, single, divorced, with or without children, entry-level, executive-level, blue-collar, professional, struggling just to get by or enjoying all the 'perks' and stresses of a top job and salary . . . [we operate] against a backdrop of shifting cultural and economic forces, many of which have been hostile to our very identity as women . . . one key reason for the working woman's lack of satisfaction is that she has been discouraged from putting her whole being, her whole feminine being, into her work."

Every walk of life needs its revolutionaries, its Vinson & Elkins, its No Glass Ceiling Task Force. It needs mentors and allies, workers willing to speak up and risk being marginalized for the chance to make permanent change. And think what would happen if the political parties—most of them filled with lawyers anyway—joined this strategy. The worlds of politics and business would finally mirror the country they serve.

The State of the State of Alabama

Just as Vinson & Elkins provides a business model for the expansion of women's leadership, the women of Alabama are doing the same in every sector for one of the poorest states in the nation.

Their bible of change is called the green book, after the color of its cover. I first heard about it at a conference on women and politics at Auburn University in 2002, where the group that created it—the Alabama Women's Initiative—spoke with enthusiasm about their recipe for radical change. And their state desperately needs it. Alabama ranks fiftieth in the United States in the number of female elected officials. Their delegation to the U.S. Congress consists only of men; the state legislature has 7.8 percent women.

Even worse, Alabama lies near the bottom in most measures for quality of life: forty-third out of fifty states in per capita income, forty-second in percentage of people living in poverty (17 percent, compared to 13 percent for America as a whole), forty-ninth in the percentage of all citizens completing high school (fiftieth when it comes to women), and forty-ninth in women's health. It ranks forty-seventh in low-birth-weight babies and forty-sixth in infant mortality—no surprise since Alabama is fiftieth in spending on all children's programs. As Republican governor Bob Riley admits, "We're last in all the things that are good, first in all the things that are bad."

Knowing the dismal state of their state, the Women's Initiative began its work (much like the White House Project) through simple arithmetic: They looked at political positions, boards (public and private), judgeships, chambers of commerce, higher education, corporations, and nonprofits—and counted the number of women in them. They laid out the case in their forty-eight-page booklet (the green book), formally called *The Status of Women in Leadership in Alabama,* linking abysmal economic conditions to the "status of women citizens." They also reminded us that the health and educational performance of children is directly linked to the health and education of the mother. A reason that Alabama is in such bad shape, they say: "Neglect of a major resource: women." The group unabashedly discusses the unique qualities of women leaders and why they are vital to the health of the democracy—inclusive decision making and team building, the tendency to mentor more fully and to listen more carefully, empowerment across lines of authority. If we want a democracy, we will put the democratic nature of women to work.

The Women's Initiative prescription for Alabama is part community activism and part personal activism: Ask any women's group to which you belong to discuss the report. Speak up. Write to the governor. Encourage qualified women to run for office, and support them. Be mindful of the numbers of women in leadership, and monitor them for the good of all. Act locally. Reach across race, class, politics, and gender. If you are already a leader, bring others along through hiring and promotion. Change the culture by challenging stereotypes.

The women of the initiative, through painstaking research and loving care, have signed on for the business of transformation, telling Alabama that increased numbers of women in leadership will change their lives. They took five thousand copies of their booklet from Hunstville to Selma, talking to garden clubs and churches, at civic and school meetings, making the issues concrete, convincing women they can be part of a political process that will shift the tectonic plates of power and poverty in their state.

When I met them, their booklet was in its second printing, and they had just started to reach younger women with a program called Leading Edge, which trains college women to travel and speak on behalf of women's leadership. Next: the girls of the Birmingham school system. Soon, I'm sure, every female in Alabama will know and support the state-saving efforts between the covers of the green book.

So Different, and Yet . . .

Could any two groups be more disparate than the women of Alabama and the lawyers of Texas? Yet they are very similar, both in their problems and in their solutions:

- One fought a glass ceiling, the other a sticky floor, and both measured the value of women's leadership in terms of a business case.
- Quality-of-life issues led to prescriptions for social intervention, be they working parent lunches or women's support groups.

- Mentoring was seen as crucial to increasing numbers and guaranteeing success.

- Both groups used media to change culture: picture-perfect in-house PowerPoint for one, a well-argued and widely distributed publication for the other.

- Whether from legal roots or grass roots, both were crystal clear about the importance of numbers. The law firm *had* to diversify or it would become an anachronism. Women in Alabama *had* to become leaders because only unique solutions would help the state out of its mess.

- Women, with male allies, were assembled to pick apart the problem and to define the solutions. The men understood that this effort was not just about women; they, too, would benefit. Male lawyers at Vinson & Elkins needed the same kind of career development, and they wanted support for parenting. When the Alabama women needed financial support, they sought out a male ally at the Alabama Power Company and he was there for them, even though his company had been identified as a problem, because it lacked women on its board.

- The next generation was on everyone's mind, for both personal and civic-minded reasons. Attorney Yeates's original motivation came from mothering later in life and realizing how badly women and men need work/life balance; Reasoner was touched by his own daughter's experience. The women of Alabama placed children on the green book cover and throughout the text to show whose future they were protecting.

- Finally, both knew they were in the business of transformation. The Alabama women named it directly, ending a large section of their report *The Impact of Women in Leadership* with a piece called "Transformational Leadership and Women." The shifts inside Vinson & Elkins have become contagious. Everyone is thinking long term—a strength of women.

Neither initiative assigned blame, but both took responsibility for future solutions. They put a larger frame around the business and around the problem, automatically creating more options. As a result, their excitement is palpable, their commitment complete, and their prospects for change irrefutable. Why? Because their circles of life—of work and of family—have been redrawn to overlap, and they have created a community where no one is alone and everyone is valued.

These initiatives are the right thing at the right time. Research conducted jointly in 2003 by the Simmons College School of Management in Boston and the Committee of 200 (a professional association of preeminent businesswomen and entrepreneurs) shows that only 9 percent of teen girls and 15 percent of teen boys intend to pursue careers in business. Most girls and some boys aspire to "make a difference in the world" and "help others," and they don't see business doing that. As the report says, "They still may not understand that business can also be a positive mechanism for social change."

And in politics, young people who volunteer in record numbers don't see themselves as future political leaders. A poll by the Panetta Institute in 2000 found that 73 percent of college students volunteered in the last two years, and most more than once. But young women who volunteer don't see politics as the place to take their leadership skills. Today's young people are becoming more liberal than the generation that preceded them, but they eschew labeling, including party labels. Even more troubling than young women opting out of political leadership is the tendency of about seven million of them (ages eighteen to twenty-four) not to vote—enough to change the course of elections.

It's Not Either/Or

A crisis-ridden state and a powerful law firm, without knowledge of each other's challenges, moved in tandem to repaint the landscapes of their cultures. They refused to accept personal and professional barriers, setting in motion sweeping change that, if fully enacted, will affect all it touches. Ability went unquestioned, authority was given and used, ambition became a group value, and everyone spoke with an authenticity that brought strength and diversity, and a culture of inclusion.

How did this happen? People of goodwill made it their business to speak up and get involved. Each group refused to accept that work and family are separate realms; work *is* family, and family *is* work. They demanded new options. They got off their mental treadmills and insisted that relational values are business values, that the work of women is the work of all, that dualistic thinking about public and private lives was getting us nowhere.

These groups grabbed at the circles of work and family and tugged them into overlap, insisting on a third sphere for every citizen, the sphere of community—a place that tends to operate invisibly because it is, by tradition, the domain of women.

What if we intentionally discarded that well-worn phrase "balancing work and family" and instead spoke of "integrating work and family," of formalizing the work of women as community builders by making it a value of both genders instead of a "third shift" for women. Women in sufficient numbers could then bring these competencies into the workplace, showing men how to participate, making women's uniqueness "good for business."

The overlap of the public and private—that place called community—is where women have traditionally honed their leadership abilities. It has been the acceptable zone in which women can exercise power and ambition, because it is an extension of our role in the family. What a false distinction. In truth, politics and business are as rich with community possibilities as any church group, as any family picnic, and they would benefit enormously from women's skills at relationship and teamwork and compromise and empathy. We must stop devaluing these integral functions, as the women of Alabama suggest and as the firm of Vinson & Elkins insists, and embrace them, which means embracing women in all realms, in all sectors, at all levels.

It is about survival. It is about women's agenda, not their gender, and the agenda is about transformation. Remember the words of Sally Helgesen in *The Female Advantage* when she said that one of the characteristics that most distinguishes women's leadership from men's is how they see their work as "encompassing a vision of society—they relate decisions to their larger effect on the role of the family, the American educational system, the environment, even world peace . . . They feel they must make a difference not just to their companies, but to the world."

Even better: Research has proved it works. The ways women lead are embraced by management consultants because they're transformational and good business practice. Employees are happier and more productive with women's style. Female legislators bring a greater variety of people into the process, expanding participatory democracy, and they focus on bills that benefit whole communities, making politics more relevant. In every sector, in every business and legislature, the power of women's work and women's values is our best hope, our best intervention, the only solution we haven't tried, and the one that is guaranteed to succeed.

It requires an insistence and persistence on the part of women (and their male allies) to get there because men will not automatically sign on. It would require abdicating power, and that's not an easy sell. We must make it known that we are ready to lead, that, in fact, we demand it, not only to fulfill the promise of democracy, but also to save it from a laundry list of ills—from companies that make parenting difficult and frustrating, from command-and-control leadership that eliminates all but a few tired solutions, from a government that ignores the *basic* security needs of its citizens. We have our minds, we have our communities, we have our votes, we have our wallets—we have our ability to influence the next generation. These are rich natural resources. Once we start mining them, leadership is inevitable.

▲ ▲ ▲

Ida B. Wells is a forerunner who also redefined leadership, like the women in Houston and Alabama. Fearless journalist, suffragist, and civil rights activist, she understood the power of voice. In 1889, she became the editor and co-owner of a local black newspaper, the *Free Speech and Headlight*. After three black store owners and friends were lynched in 1892, she attacked the hangings in print, encouraging black citizens of Memphis to boycott white-owned businesses. As a result, her newspaper office was destroyed.

Wells escaped with only her life to Chicago, where she continued to write and organize into the twentieth century. At one point she returned to the South to visit a group of black men who had been sentenced to death for defending themselves against white attackers. She found they had given up hope, so they sang spirituals about death and a better world beyond. Enraged, Wells demanded they affirm life in their music because they needed to fight to live. They did both—and they were freed.

Gloria Steinem often asks her audiences to perform one outrageous act a day. Eleanor Roosevelt, of another generation, suggested we should continually scare ourselves by our choices and actions. For myself, I point again to that old English definition of courage: Speak your mind by telling all your heart. If we combine them all—if we speak our minds about women's leadership, making outrageous demands for change even if it frightens us—we will be singing for our lives again. At first it might be a solo act, but over time, as the fear fades and more people join, we'll find ourselves in harmony. Choirs will follow until, finally, we hear both the blend of many and the sweet contribution of the individual. The leadership gap becomes the leadership glut. We are *all* running the world. As it should be.

9

Never "know your place." Never "shrink to fit."

—Geraldine Laybourne, chairman and CEO, Oxygen Media

In the process of writing, I contacted some of our greatest natural resources—women in leadership—to refine my perspective, and to add advice and inspiration about the future. The response was swift and overwhelming; I wish I could print every word from these amazing women. I had originally intended to sprinkle their quotes throughout the book, but when I saw them together, I realized their power lay in their interconnections. Though this book mostly deals with the change we need in systems and institutions, it is illuminating to see the personal strategies of today's leaders. Here are the two questions I asked, and an edited selection of the responses.

- What were your biggest obstacles to attaining leadership, and what helped you most to overcome them?

- If you could give leadership advice to the generation that will ultimately replace you, what would
  it be?

The Obstacles

In my early years, it was my own sense of ambivalence about resolving femininity and authority. Later, it was thinking about whether I
could have a family and an army career (mobility gives children and
work a whole new dimension of challenge).

—Lt. General Claudia J. Kennedy (Ret.),
first female three-star general in the U.S. Army

Speak too forcefully and you are considered overbearing; speak softly,
and you are considered to have no opinion. It's the scenario of being
considered pushy or a pushover.

—Connie Duckworth, founder,
Eight Wings Enterprises LLC;
chair of the Committee of 200

Some people—women as well as men—accept very assertive and even
arrogant behavior from a man, but expect a woman to be deferential
and reassuring. It's hard to be hard-driving, visionary—and deferential!

—Joan Williams, professor of law and director of the
Program on Gender, Work & Family, American University

As I grew up, I learned that the way I present myself—"command
bearing," some call it—has a lot to do with those intangibles that
help people "see" the leader in you at the outset. Such things include

a confident voice, good posture, the ability to use eye contact, and a good handshake.

—Kate Dernocoeur, explorer

Women's leadership means doing what needs to be done without waiting to ask for permission.

—Diane Rosenfeld,
law professor, Harvard University

It is a woman thing to think that "aggressive" is bad. I know what I mean by leadership: speaking out, taking risks, being aggressive, being compassionate, assuming responsibility for exercising the power that each of us has, overcoming one's fears and anxieties. All that is leadership.

—Simone Joyaux,
ACFRE, Joyaux Associates

Getting an MBA helped me psychologically to feel on a par with the boys on the board, whatever board it was. Being a confident public speaker is a necessary part of leadership—but it is learned through experience.

—Marion Ballard, board of directors,
Washington Area Women's Foundation

To compensate, I worked harder than others and walked the talk by delivering bottom-line results. I developed dependencies in my trade by pioneering niches.

—Ruth Ann Marshall, president,
North America Region of Mastercard International

The obstacle that comes to mind most is what might be called a "lack of vision." This played out with superiors not necessarily believing I could take the next step.

—*Hildy Simmons, managing director,*
JP Morgan Private Bank, Global Foundations Group

First, there were certainly the stereotypes I had to (and still) confront being an Asian woman. We shouldn't fool ourselves. Those stereotypes of Asian women as submissive, passive, or inconsequential still exist, and even more strongly the higher up you go. I overcome this challenge by being visible and outspoken. I've made a commitment to speaking dozens of times every year to all kinds of people across the country on why it's necessary for us to become a more culturally "fluent," internationally aware nation. Often I am the first Asian-American woman that they have ever seen take the podium to keynote, and that always shocks me. But I've learned that once people get used to the image of power embodied in different kinds of people, change begins. Until we have more Asian-Americans in public leadership positions—in our corporations, in the Beltway and local government, and in the public eye in general—I know I will continue to face stereotypes. Consistent presence is key.

—*Phoebe Eng, author of* Warrior Lessons *and change strategist*

I was always underestimated (I think probably because I'm a woman and Latin). Even when I had established a very successful Latin-American business, it took a long time (much longer than I think it would have taken for an Anglo guy . . . all other things being equal) to get to run our U.S. business.

—*Maria Elena Lagomasino, chair and*
CEO, JP Morgan Private Bank

Initially there was skepticism that I could do the job, handle the pressure and tough decision making, and command the respect of subordinates and adversaries. When I first looked for a job as a lawyer a number of years back, I actually heard partners say things like, "You seem very bright, but I'm not sure our clients will accept you." I was almost denied an appointment to a major bar committee because I was "too Asian and a woman." When I was up for a general counsel position, a male decision maker said to another (who happened to be a woman who knew me well, unbeknownst to him), "You don't want that little girl to be your lawyer, do you?" (I should mention that I am what most would call diminutive.) Fortunately, she said, "I most certainly do!" And her opinion was shared by the others and led to my accepting the position.

—Diane Yu, chief of staff and deputy to the president,
New York University; chair of the American Bar Association
Commission on Women in the Profession

One of the most difficult tasks for women is overcoming the "imposter syndrome"—the feeling that we aren't good enough, don't have the necessary background, or don't deserve leadership opportunities. We feel like we need one more credential, one more bit of experience, et cetera. Men do not have this problem. They take the job and figure out how to do it later. We need to adopt some of their sense of entitlement to leadership.

—Martha Burk, cofounder and president of the
Center for Advancement of Public Policy;
chair of the National Council of Women's Organizations

Know thyself, or make your best guess, then you will naturally gravitate toward the people who will appreciate your gifts. Obstacles come in the form of people and institutions that are antithetical to your personal goals.

—Caryn Mandabach, partner,
Carsey-Werner-Mandabach independent television studio

My biggest obstacle was not knowing how "the system" worked. What helped was not being afraid to ask questions . . . I have found people to generally be very willing to share their personal experiences.

—Marsha J. Evans, president and CEO, American Red Cross

My biggest obstacle was not being an extrovert and keeping my head down and doing my job, not looking up at where I wanted to go next.

—Patricia Fili-Krushel,
executive vice president of administration,
Time Warner

The biggest obstacles became apparent when I went to medical school and, subsequently, during my terms in academia and in administration. Those obstacles were gender and racial (ethnic) discrimination that were manifest both overtly and covertly. Additionally, the sharing of power with females in medicine was enormously difficult for the institution and for many of the men in power. As an example, although we currently have a fantastic woman as president of the university, we have never had a female chair of any department in the medical school. Power differential, in my opinion, presents a real obstacle to the progress of women.

—Jean G. Spaulding, trustee, the Duke Endowment

The biggest obstacles for me probably came from my Asian-American heritage, as opposed to my female one. There were so few role models of Asian-American women leaders for me to look up to and emulate. I felt like I had to make it up as I went along. That said, because I was the oldest child in a family of girls, my parents always insisted I could do anything a man could do. And my sisters would probably tell you that being the boss came quite naturally to me.

—*Jeannie Park, executive editor,* People *magazine*

One of the challenges women have in attaining a leadership position is getting themselves into the right 'pre-position,' so that when opportunity finally presents itself, they can step right into the job. I worked for eight years at the National Basketball Association, with responsibilities that included a host of projects relating to women's basketball and direct contact with Commissioner David Stern and Deputy Commissioner Russ Granik. So when the WNBA came into being in 1996, I was in a prime spot to move into the president's role.

—*Val Ackerman, president,*
the Women's National Basketball Association

The Advice

Don't ever agree to take on a leadership role for the money, power, title, or prestige; take on the role because you have a passion for the cause.

—*Colleen Barrett, president and COO, Southwest Airlines*

Always tell those above you what you are interested in doing. Pursue jobs avidly. Never assume that the bosses surely must *know* that you're interested in something, or that you're the *obvious* choice for it—and never assume they'd *never* pick you either. The men around you are far likelier to be seeing themselves in the job above them, and to be making their case, energetically—and this counts, when you're looking to make a hire, or a promotion. Take yourself seriously, picture yourself rising to the top and make your case . . . Along the way, steadfastly watch for opportunities to make the case to others about individual women (and young people, and people of color) and the strengths they bring—strengths more traditional bosses may be missing themselves, and therefore may be unable to recognize as strengths.

—*Geneva Overholser, endowed chair,*
Missouri School of Journalism; former editor of the
Des Moines Register; *former ombudsman of the* Washington Post

If you struggle with shyness and self-consciousness, keep reaching beyond what is comfortable, and surround yourself with a few key women who will cheer you on, listen to the ups and downs, and encourage you toward your greatest dreams for leadership. Know that your thoughts and perspectives matter. Support the women around you as they reach for their dreams and speak out, just as they support you. Make a commitment to each other, and set up regular times to check in and support each other. You will surprise yourself with what becomes possible.

—*Cathy Salser, executive director, A Window Between Worlds*

Never listen to anyone who tells you that the odds are against you. You are an independent variable . . . Stay physically fit for two reasons: One, It gives you the stamina you need for your career, which is a marathon, not a sprint. Two, A fit woman has more public and professional credibility. Fair? No. But that's how strong image is on perceptions of power.

—Lt. General Claudia J. Kennedy (Ret.),
first female three-star general in the U.S. Army

Speak up for yourself. Ask for what you want. If there is a leadership position in which you are interested, seek it proactively. If you don't ask, you don't always get!

—Ellen Auster, New York tristate tax partner,
Deloitte & Touche LLP

If you fail to think consciously in terms of building toward a leadership position, you're unlikely to achieve it.

—Ellen Chesler, director of the Program on Reproductive Health
and Rights, Soros Foundations Networks; author of Woman of Valor:
Margaret Sanger and the Birth Control Movement in America

Be ethical, inclusive of all, respectful of those who went ahead, and gutsy.

—Elisabeth Griffith, headmistress,
the Madeira School, author of
In Her Own Right: The Life of Elizabeth Cady Stanton

Be patient with change and never give up. People want to participate in change and have as much control as possible over events in which they take part. So create opportunities for that. Have a clear purpose for yourself that's meaningful . . . Communicate goals so that others can connect to their meaning.

—Beatrice Harris, managing partner, Harris Rothenberg

Ascribe to what First Lady Eleanor Roosevelt says: "Do something to scare yourself today." In other words, take a risk, try something new, move out of your comfort zone and feel the exhilaration of power when you succeed and embrace the learning when you don't.

—*Teresa L. Cavanagh, senior vice president and*
director, Women Entrepreneurs' Connection, Fleet Bank

Start to envision yourself and conduct yourself as already having the power and influence you are striving for. It will come.

—*Susan Butler, former managing partner, Accenture*

Take risks. You need to actively, every single day, do something that makes you uncomfortable so that you learn the value of that experience and you learn not to let it paralyze you. If you are not willing to take a risk, some white man will and you will lose the opportunity. That's how simple it is.

—*Jane D. Pigott, senior partner,*
Winston & Strawn

Never accept "NO." Be persistent! When the door is closed, look for a window! You never know where you will encounter help. You may find an opening anywhere, even in the most unlikely places. Empower yourself with worth.

—*Camille Ferrara, development associate,*
the Committee for Hispanic Children and Families, Inc.

Mentoring has to ebb and flow between the generations. There are no more gurus; but there are good experiences that happen to all of us wherever we are, and these can be a rich source of cross-generational learning.

—*Shifra Bronznick, principal, Bronznick Jacoby, LLC*

Be proactive in asking for new roles and great responsibility. As women, we often assume that performance will speak for itself—if I do a good job, it will be recognized and rewarded. While this is sometimes the case, you can't assume it. If you feel you are ready for the next level or a career-broadening assignment, ask for it. Be prepared to make a case for why it makes sense for you and the organization.

—*Francesca Brockett, executive vice president,*
strategic planning and business development, Toys "R" Us

Figure out the person you want to be before you decide on the leadership role you want. If you become the person you've always wanted as a leader, you will become that leader.

—*Ginny Corsi, management consultant,*
Corsi Associates

Be yourself and don't compromise by trying to be someone you are not. If you find yourself somewhere where you are not being recognized for your work and getting the opportunities you want, move on. There is always some place that will.

—*Marley Kaplan, president and CEO,*
Chess-in-the-Schools

You will occasionally be faced with a situation where everyone around you is trying to convince you that the traffic light is green when you see it as red. Take a deep breath and follow your own instincts.

         —*Susan Ness, former commissioner of the*
         Federal Communications Commission

Don't ever let anyone stop you from doing your work, and know that they can't stop you unless you let them. They can deny you jobs, resources, all sorts of things. But they can't stop you from doing your work. If they put an insurmountable roadblock in your way, gather your resources and slide around it from another direction.

         —*The Reverend Dr. Katherine Hancock Ragsdale,*
         Religious Coalition for Reproductive Choice

Withdraw your need for approval from external sources and anoint yourself with your own approval. Take it back. Reclaim your intuitive, exquisite self. It will be your ticket to a true and lasting deeper wisdom.

         —*Jody Weiss, founder, PeaceKeeper Products*

Be comfortable and secure with yourself . . . others will flock to you.

         —*Jennifer Blei Stockman, national co-chair of the*
         Republican Pro-Choice Coalition

Define your own top five personal priorities and stay centered on them no matter what comes along to distract or derail you (including men).

         —*Kathleen M. Lingle, national work/life director, KPMG LLP*

Be authentic. Understand how to communicate so that you can be heard. Then communicate, communicate, communicate.

> —*Lauren M. Doliva, managing partner,*
> *Global E-business Practice, Heidrick & Struggles International Inc.*

A true leader is one who leads with enthusiasm, courage, and faith. Integrity is key. We need people who lead from not only their heads but from their hearts.

> —*Helene Lerner, president,*
> *Creative Expansions Inc.*

Get the finest general education, learn languages, travel the world, develop cultural interests, think globally, amass negotiating skills, understand the responsibilities of leadership.

> —*Jeanette Wagner, marketing and management consultant,*
> *former vice chair, Estee Lauder Cosmetics*

Future, as well as present leaders, must really see that leadership does not reside on some pinnacle but that it lives on a broad, wide plane that is big enough for many.

> —*Friedrike Merck, philanthropist*

Take time to get to know people around you; build relationships because in the end, this is what gets the job done and makes you happy along the way.

> —*Jackie Barnes, chief operating officer,*
> *Girl Scouts of the USA*

Have two mentors: one for professional development, one for personal development . . . Always say yes to life. Take risks and seek out new opportunities always . . . sometimes your avocation might become your vocation . . . build upon the skills you have and develop new ones *constantly* . . . take classes and seminars, even if they do not apply to your work . . . learn, learn, learn . . . from everyone . . . Most of all be good to yourself; reward yourself when you have done well . . . even if someone else does not . . .

—Martha Madden, corporate vice president
of business development, Tetra Tech, Inc.

Remember that every employee brings value to the company. Some of the best ideas just might come from the receptionist.

—Joan Gerberding, president, Nassau Media Partners;
national president and foundation chair,
American Women in Radio and Television

Always do your best and work not only on your job but also on expanding your skills. Writing, public speaking, group facilitation/ negotiation, and how to deal with difficult people are some particular skills that are useful regardless of profession. Have a positive attitude. People are much more likely to want you on their team and follow you if you are positive and energetic.

—Marsha J. Evans, president and CEO, American Red Cross

Form a network of women who work who are your good friends. Do business with them as often as you can.

—Jewelle W. Bickford, senior managing director,
Capital Markets Group, Rothschild North America

To be a truly successful manager, whenever people come to see you, give them the impression that they could change your mind. Be it a conversation with your boss, co-worker, an employee—one benefit of going into a discussion in this frame of mind is that it actually does keep you open to new ideas and new ways of looking at things. It also keeps you from looking (and acting) like you know it all; it will cultivate your reputation for being a good listener (you'll hear a lot more about what's really happening), for being open to new ideas, and for being able to see the big picture.

—Darcy Bingham, cofounder,
San Diego Social Venture Partners

Leadership shouldn't end in the workplace. Leaders must help make the world a better place by giving back to their community.

—Lillian Vernon, founding chair,
Lillian Vernon Corporation

Have this idea in the back of your head and then in the front of your head that what you're doing really matters and it's important to you to do it, that you're going to figure out a way to get it done.

—Judy Woodruff, anchor and
senior correspondent, CNN

You are not your job. You are filling a job, hopefully building a career—but fulfillment must come through the quality of choices you make in your life . . . Money and power, unto themselves, have little meaning.

—Loreen Arbus, president and
executive producer, Loreen Arbus Productions Inc.

Once you get to the higher levels, it is not so much about competence, since most people at high levels are competent. It is more about connections, networks, mentors, et cetera, who can help you achieve your goals and overcome obstacles.

—Kimberly Till, vice president,
Media and Entertainment, Microsoft

Each day I try to give lessons from my elder [her grandaunt and mentor], Bazoline, to the women of tomorrow. They must know that the lessons of leadership are bound in the development of community and the experiences of family. They must watch and listen to the lessons of leadership before them, even after being educated in the best schools. If they watch and listen, they will find that it is the common sense of collaborative, supportive work that makes for strong families, balance, and achievement at work.

—Jane E. Smith, CEO,
Business and Professional Women/USA

Acknowledgments

In the fall of 1997, Susan Berresford, president of the Ford Foundation, introduced me to Connie Buchanan, the new program officer in religion. I had known of Connie through her work at the Harvard Divinity School, where she founded the program for women's studies in religion. Allison Bernstein, also at Ford, lent me her treasured copy of Connie's book, *Choosing to Lead: Women and the Crisis of American Values.*

And that is how it started. Connie, through writing and conversation, convinced me that women had to both knock on powerful doors and sit at the tables of power. Her brilliance, though she may not know it, was the impetus behind the creation of the White House Project and, ultimately, this book.

Allison also led me to Ellen Schall, of New York University, who showed me a stunning piece of research, "The Paradox of Post Heroic Leadership" by Joyce Fletcher of Simmons College. Reading Joyce's work, I understood that organizations, if they have any hope of transforming their workplaces, must learn to value the relational strengths identified with women. Her thinking is a building block of this book.

As Peggy McIntosh of Wellesley College has said, the leader is only the tip of the iceberg: "Underneath is the collaborative subtext of life, the numerous, countless acts of enabling, supporting, facilitating, and creating conditions under which 'tips' of icebergs can break through the surface." And so I want to acknowledge the iceberg that kept this book afloat:

First, my life partner and in-house editor, Nancy Lee. Nancy worked with me nights and weekends for nine months, lending her enormous writing and editing skills to the project. During this time (and illustrating how work and family are integrated), she also kept up with her day job as a vice president at the *New York Times,* planned a beautiful wedding for our oldest son, helped our two daughters get settled in New York City, and kept food in the refrigerator. This book would not have happened without her love and support.

The talented and trusted former director of research at the White House Project, Shauna Shames, served as my primary researcher. It was Shauna who called with excitement to discuss an important concept she had formulated: the growing influence of a third sphere— community—formed as the private and public spheres increasingly overlapped. Shauna's 2001 graduate thesis from Harvard first fueled my understanding of how early feminists expanded their reach into public roles, cleverly manipulating the power they had in their narrow private sphere of influence. I'm sure Shauna's leadership will be felt across the country in the years ahead.

Melissa Silverstein, a driving force a decade ago in Take Our Daughters to Work at the Ms. Foundation for Women, teaches me continually about the power of culture to make change. Melissa heavily influenced the culture chapter of this book and many chapters in the life of this work. But even more important to me, she was the first person to insist I write what I had learned through the years about women's leadership. She even gave me a blank book for my thoughts.

My associate Helen French exemplifies post heroic leadership. A highly competent woman who keeps people and projects connected, she also reminds me daily of the meaning and vision of our work. Helen embodies the often-unsung relational skills that women provide in work and family. Women like her are the real glue of leadership.

The executive directors of both the Ms. Foundation for Women (Sara Gould) and of the White House Project (Beverly Neufeld) enrich our work with their vision and perseverance. They have been true partners. Shifra Bronznick, a consultant and friend, clarified my thinking (and my life) with her research and practice on women's leadership. Wendy Puriefoy, longtime friend and former board chair of the Ms. Foundation, and Barbara Dobkin, an amazing activist and philanthropist, made the very existence of the White House Project possible.

Kathleen Hall Jamieson, former dean of the Annenberg School for Communication at the University of Pennsylvania, framed the core of the White House Project mission. Her thinking informed a good deal of the research in the book, as did that of Celinda Lake, of Lake Snell Perry & Associates, who conducted much of the polling, some alongside Linda DiVall and Bob Carpenter of American Viewpoint. Tom Cosgrove was the architect of our first straw poll, "Twenty Women Who Could Lead America," and Walter Anderson of *Parade* magazine and his successor, Lee Kravitz, made it possible for us to introduce these women to millions of Americans. Page Gardner steered the White House Project's important work documenting the absence of women from the Sunday shows and our "Barriers and Opportunities" research. Ann Burroughs joined together important national and international players in women's political leadership during our "Why Women Matter" summit.

Many young women of all races and regions have interned at the White House Project. They stood up, stayed up, and took the time to educate me about their views on women and leadership. I hope I proved a good student.

My oldest son, Gene, did much of the smart framing around Joyce Fletcher's work, and my two daughters, Kirsten and Renée, both feminist scholars, added wisdom and cheer throughout. My friends across the country continued to love me through months of limited contact. Perhaps they were luckier than those close by—Vin Alabiso and Pam

Tibbetts—who listened to more chatter about women's leadership than I'm sure they could stand yet still added enormously to my thinking and sanity.

My agent, Andrew Wylie, believed in the book, and in me, from day one with very little history to back it up. He helped me get the editor I wanted—Janet Goldstein at Viking Penguin—who shaped a well-intentioned manuscript by a nonwriter into a book I'm proud to own.

To those I interviewed and to those who sent me their thoughts on leadership: You are the final chapter of the book but the first chapter in our efforts to close the leadership gap. Thank you.

Finally, I want to acknowledge the late Bella Abzug. She would be amused to find me so deeply involved in political parity, since it was not my primary focus while she was alive (much to her loud consternation). When I started the book, I tacked a large picture of her over my workstation as a reminder of her unswerving dedication to women and to democracy. Her spirit is deeply embedded here. She was truly ahead of her time.

Notes

Introduction: It's About Time

Page

xii   **Of 435:** For statistics on women in politics, see the Web site of the Center for American Women and Politics at Rutgers University: www.cawp.rutgers.edu.

xii   **Women are nearly:** Bureau of Labor Statistics, Department of Labor, www.bls.gov, 2002.

xii   **yet we:** Catalyst, www.catalystwomen.org, 2001 (corporate officers: 2002 data).

xii   **Internationally:** For statistics on women in international politics, see the Web site for the Inter-Parliamentary Union: www.ipu.org, as of November 10, 2003.

xii   **Norway:** *New York Times,* July 14, 2003.

xii   **the "cultural ideal":** Constance H. Buchanan, *Choosing to Lead: Women and the Crisis of American Values.*

xiii   *numbers matter:* Rosabeth Moss Kanter, *Men and Women of the Corporation.*

xv   **the women of South Africa:** From the White House Project's *Why Women Matter* presentations at the National Press Club, Washington, D.C., March 3, 2003, and at the Crowne Plaza Hotel, San Francisco, March 6, 2003.

xv   **The African National:** Inter-Parliamentary Union, *op. cit.*

xvii   **John Naisbitt:** John Naisbitt, *Megatrends.*

Chapter 1: Why Women Matter

2   **In July 2003:** *San Jose Mercury News,* July 23, 2003.

2   **In the words of Anne Sweeney:** Transcript of a national talk radio show, *Saper Says,* hosted by Nanci Saper, March 8, 2002.

3 **"This is the great":** Margaret Heffernan, "The Female CEO ca. 2002," *Fast Company,* August 2002.

3 **woman starting a business:** Harriet Rubin, *Fast Company,* January 2000.

3 **families with stay-at-home fathers:** Julie Shields, "More U.S. Dads Balance Laptops, Kids on Laps," www.womensenews. org, June 15, 2003.

4 **Women are 51 percent:** Bureau of Labor Statistics, *op. cit.*

4 **"second shift":** Arlie Russell Hochschild with Anne Machung, *The Second Shift: Working Parents and the Revolution At Home.*

4 **More than 60 percent:** Bureau of Labor Statistics, 2002, *op. cit.*

4 **but we're still responsible:** Katha Pollitt, "US: Feminism Lite," *Le Monde diplomatique,* July 17, 2003.

4 **"status of legend":** Rubin, *op. cit.*

4 **If you take:** Business and Professional Women/USA's "Workplace Facts & Figures Sheet," www.bpwusa.org, 2002.

4 **We sit on:** Catalyst, 2003.

4 **top five wage earners:** Catalyst, 1998.

4 **world of nonprofits:** *New York Times,* June 2, 2001.

4 **Of nearly 12,000:** Historical statistics from the Center for American Women and Politics, *op. cit.*

7 **With tongue in cheek:** The NAB radio show Web site, 2001.

7 **I found out:** *Inside Women's Power: Learning from Leaders,* Wellesley College and Winds of Change Foundation, 2001.

8 **Now male CEOs:** Daniel Goleman, *Emotional Intelligence.*

10 **"Nobody fought":** Barbara Mikulski et al., *Nine and Counting.*

10 **"We developed":** *ibid.*

10 **"It wasn't that":** *ibid.*

11 **"Numbers matter":** From the White House Project's *Why Women Matter* presentation at the National Press Club, Washington, D.C., March 3, 2003.

11 **Recent research:** Amy Caiazza, "Does Women's Representation in Elected Office Lead to Women-Friendly Policy?," Institute for Women's Policy Research, 2002; Sue Thomas and Susan Welch, "The Impact of Women in State Legislatures: Numerical and Organizational Strength," in *The Impact of Women in Public Office,* Sue Carroll, ed., Indiana University Press, 2001.

11 **15 percent of legislators:** Kanter, *op cit.* (Kanter's classic nu-

merical theory of tokens within an institution, first put forward in 1977, shows that when one group is 15 percent or less of a body, its status as token greatly constrains its behavior. I have applied it here to legislators, though Kanter's writing discusses only corporations.)

11   **Women now hold:** Inter-Parliamentary Union, *op. cit.,* as of October 2, 2003.

11   **Wales recently reached:** *Guardian Unlimited,* www.guardian. co.uk, May 9, 2003.

12   **Women in seven European countries:** "UN: Women Gain in Political Clout, Lag in Schooling," www.womensenews.org, May 30, 2003.

12   **women are bringing fresh perspectives:** Swanee Hunt and Cristina Posa, *Toronto Star,* December 2, 2001.

12   **The United Nations:** Swanee Hunt and Cristina Posa, "Women Waging Peace," *Foreign Policy,* May/June 2001.

13   **"For generations":** From the Women Waging Peace Web site, www.womenwagingpeace.org.

14   **After the amendment passed:** Pippa Norris, *Electoral Engineering.*

15   **nearly on top in women's political:** Inter-Parliamentary Union, *op. cit.*

Chapter 2: Barriers to Leadership

17   **Many traits:** Deborah L. Rhode, *Speaking of Sex.*

17   **Eighty-seven percent of Americans:** Gallup poll, May 2003.

17   **Seventy-six percent of "influential Americans":** Roper ASW poll, February 2003.

17   **If the 2004 elections was held today:** Omnibus survey conducted by Lake Snell Perry & Associates, May 8–19, 2003.

18   **"the 'no problem' problem":** Rhode, *op. cit.*

18   **"Americans have a curiously":** Katha Pollitt, "Feminism's Unfinished Business," *Atlantic Online,* November 1997.

19   **Shirley Franklin:** Speech at Emory University, 2002, Eric Rangus, erangus@emory.edu.

21 **If, for instance, the pipeline:** Center for American Women and Politics, *op. cit.*

21 **Half of our top:** *Young Elected Leaders Project,* Eagleton Institute, Rutgers University, 2003.

21 **top leadership in business:** "Women Wow! Facts 2003," Business Women's Network Diversity Best Practices Web site, www.diversitybestpractices.com.

22 **"cultural ideal":** Buchanan, *op. cit.*

22 **"Most Americans believe":** Rhode, *op. cit.*

24 **"second shift":** Hochschild, *op. cit.*

24 **A 2002 study:** "Highlights of the 2002 National Study of the Changing Workforce," Families and Work Institute.

24 **"To equalize the standings":** Pollitt, *op. cit.*

25 **This deal was institutionalized:** Buchanan, *op. cit.*

25 **documented extensively:** Alexis de Tocqueville, *Democracy in America.*

25 **(mostly in jobs earning):** U.S. Census of 2000, www.census.gov.

25 **"cultural ideal":** Buchanan, *op. cit.*

26 **Ultimately her compensation:** Blanche Wiesen Cook, *Eleanor Roosevelt: 1884–1933, Vol. 1.*

26 **pushed women's concerns:** Robin Gerber, *Leadership the Eleanor Roosevelt Way.*

27 **"a masterpiece of Presidential leadership":** David M. Kennedy, *Freedom from Fear: The American People in Depression and War, 1929–1945.*

27 **Her sponsored radio program gave listeners:** Gerber, *op. cit.*

28 **"no one seems":** *New York Times,* November 3, 2003.

29 **In the original:** *New York Times,* May 15, 2003.

29 **As feminist theorist bell hooks:** *ibid.*

30 **Take Abigail Adams:** Adams letters, The Liz Library, www.thelizlibrary.org.

Chapter 3: Authority

33 **"masculinity of authority":** Buchanan, *op. cit.*

34 **According to a 2003 newspaper:** *The Guardian,* July 4, 2003.

35   **"It doesn't matter":** Eleanor Clift and Tom Brazaitis, *Madam President.*

35   **In 1984, when Geraldine:** *Denver Post,* July 16, 1984.

35   **"Dole prepares":** *New York Times,* March 11, 1999.

35   **Both Rutgers:** *Style Over Substance: Newspaper Coverage of Female Candidates: Spotlight on Elizabeth Dole,* the White House Project, 2000; Caroline Heldman, Susan J. Carroll, and Stephanie Olson, *Gender Differences in Print Media Coverage of Presidential Candidates: Elizabeth Dole's Bid for the Republican Nomination,* Rutgers University, American Political Science Association, 2000.

43   **"Kaptur can't":** *Roll Call,* March 15, 2001.

43   **It's been an uphill battle:** Buchanan, *op. cit.*

44   **Religion:** Buchanan, *op. cit.*

44   **Early suffragists:** Aileen Kraditor, *The Ideas of the Women Suffrage Movement.*

44   **The powerful temperance movement:** Buchanan, *op. cit.*

44   **"a founder of":** *ibid.*

45   **In fact, it was:** *ibid.*

45   **Unlike Europe:** Steven D. Stark, "Gap Politics," *Atlantic Monthly,* July 1996.

45   **"cultural norms of authority":** Buchanan, *op. cit.*

45   **"community service":** Theda Skocpol in "Gap Politics"; Stark, *op. cit.*

45   **alcohol-related:** *DRIVEN* magazine, Spring 2000.

45   **Senator Barbara:** *Nine and Counting, op. cit.*

46   **Governor Jennifer Granholm:** Jonathan Cohn, "Gender Bender," *New Republic,* October 14, 2002.

46   **Her platform:** *ibid.*

46   **"take back this state":** *New York Times,* August 8, 2002.

46   **"sincere whispers":** *ibid.*

46   **She defeated her Republican opponent:** Cohn, *op. cit.*

46   **"Life's most dazzling":** Michigan governor's office Web site, www.michigan.gov.

47   **Governor Kathleen Sebelius:** Cohn, *op. cit.*

47   **Governor Janet Napolitano:** *ibid.*

48   **women's team:** Gail Evans, *She Wins, You Win.*

49   **"from the foot":** Ronald A. Heifetz, *Leadership Without Easy Answers.*

49 **"in the context"**: *ibid.*

50 **Consider the strategy**: *Boston Globe,* September 23, 2003.

Chapter 4: Ambition

53 **"Raise your hands"**: Amy Finnerty, *O* magazine, September 2001.

54 **Even normally**: Bill Keller, *New York Times,* November 2, 2002.

55 **"one of the most"**: *O* magazine, *ibid.*

55 **"with a spectacular"**: *New York Times* via *O* magazine, September 2001.

55 **"Her departure"**: *ibid.*

57 **"baked cookies"**: Michael Barone, *U.S. News & World Report,* March 30, 1992.

57 **By September 1992**: *New York Times,* September 24, 1992.

57 **"viewed Mrs. Clinton"**: *New York Times,* July 13, 1992.

57 **It didn't stop**: Christopher John Farley, *Time,* April 26, 1993.

57 **"the most powerful"**: PBS timeline of the Clinton health care plan, www.pbs.org.

58 **"the resistance"**: Hillary Rodham Clinton, *Living History.*

58 **"She's pioneering"**: *New York Times,* September 24, 1992.

58 **"Let Hillary Be Hillary"**: Joyce Purnick, *New York Times,* July 15, 1994.

59 **"choiceless choice"**: Mary Catherine Bateson, *With a Daughter's Eye.*

60 **"It's not testosterone"**: Michael S. Kimmel, "What About the Boys?," Michigan Feminist Studies 14, 1999–2000.

61 **This point is underscored**: Gary F. Moncrief, Peverill Squire, and Malcolm E. Jewell, *Who Runs for the Legislature?*

66 **"The time is ripe"**: *Parade* magazine, February 1999 (all quotes).

67 **the first year**: Blanche Wiesen Cook, *Eleanor Roosevelt: 1933–1938, Vol. 2.*

67 **"Only women in power"**: *ibid.*

67 **(all men)**: Patricia Sellers, *Fortune* magazine, October 20, 2003.

68 **"Young women"**: *USA Today,* April 10, 2003.

69 **"She becomes":** Brenda Wineapple, introduction to *The Scarlet Letter* by Nathaniel Hawthorne.

Chapter 5: Ability

71 **early history:** Ann Crittenden, *The Price of Motherhood.*

73 **"identified a":** Wellesley study, *op. cit.*

75 **"excellent":** *New York Times,* May 11, 2001.

75 **They voted:** Associated Press, May 10, 2001.

76 **In research:** *Keys to the Governor's Office* study, Barbara Lee Family Foundation, 2001.

76 **she said:** Mary S. Hartman, ed. *Talking Leadership.*

76 **"I have":** *Bartleby's Quotations,* www.bartleby.com, as quoted by Letty Cottin Pogrebin in *Family Politics: Love and Power on an Intimate Frontier* (New York: McGraw-Hill, 1983).

78 **It's no better in Britain:** The *Herald,* Glasgow, Scotland, January 22, 2003.

78 **"focus group":** *Keys to the Governor's Office* study, *op. cit.*

79 **we learn:** Virginia Valian, *Why So Slow?*

80 **In the words of Haris Silajdzic:** *Women Waging Peace* Web site, www.womenwagingpeace.org.

81 **Ambassador Swanee:** Thane Peterson, "What if Women Ran the World?" *BusinessWeek Online,* April 15, 2003.

82 **"While most":** Hunt and Posa, *Foreign Policy,* May/June 2001, *op. cit.*

83 **"human security":** Jessica Tuchman Mathews, *Foreign Affairs,* January/February 1997.

84 **The report explores:** Survey research for "A Women's Len's on Global Issues: A Three Year Report, 1998 to 2001," Aspen Institute's Global Interdependence Initiative housed at the Rockefeller Brothers Fund.

84 **You won't be surprised:** "Connecting Women in the U.S. and Global Issues," a report of survey research for "A Women's Lens on Global Issues," Aspen Institute, May 2000.

84 **A new book:** Curt Weeden, *How Women Can Beat Terrorism.*

85 **The United Nations Security:** Michelle Landsberg, *Ms.* magazine, summer 2003.

86   **The European Parliament:** Hunt and Posa, *op. cit.*

86   **In our own country:** Congresswoman Eddie B. Johnson, "Women Are Crucial to Iraq Peacemaking," www.womensenews. org, July 11, 2003.

87   **"We're just like":** Shauna Curphey, www.womensenews.org, March 22, 2003.

87   **Today there are:** Nancy Gibbs, *Time,* March 24, 2003.

87   **140,000:** U.S. Army Reserve Web site, www.army.mil, updated October 1, 2003.

87   **one in seven:** Gibbs, *op. cit.*

87   **yet only 33:** *USA Today,* January 11, 2002.

87   **One level down:** Women's Research and Education Institute, "Women in the Military: Where They Stand," report by Captain Lory Manning, USN (ret.), and Vanessa R. Wight, 2000.

87   **shot, captured:** Curphy, *op. cit.*

87   **Her quote, etched on a glass panel:** *ibid.*

88   **More than 140:** *New York Times,* June 20, 2003.

88   **One woman:** *New York Times,* March 26, 2003.

88   **"Widespread sexual":** Lt. General Claudia J. Kennedy (Ret.), *Ms.* magazine, summer 2003.

88   **During the summer:** *New York Times,* June 20, 2003, *op. cit.*

88   **Later in the summer:** *New York Times,* August 29, 2003.

89   **A recent study:** ABC News, www.abcnews.com, May 19, 2003.

91   **distributed buzzers:** *USA Today,* January 21, 2002.

Chapter 6: Authenticity

95   **"Don't compromise":** Creative Quotations Web site, www. creativequotations.com.

96   **Social psychologist:** Alice H. Eagly and Blair T. Johnson, "Gender and Leadership Style: A Meta-Analysis," *Psychological Bulletin,* v. 108, no. 2, 1990.

97   **"Traditional standards of masculinity":** Hartman, *op. cit.*

100   **"Because most caretakers are female":** Elizabeth Debold, presentation to the board of directors, Ms. Foundation for Women, February 20, 2003.

102   **What does it mean to be a man?:** Michael S. Kimmel, pre-

sentation to the board of directors, Ms. Foundation for Women, February 21, 2003.

103   **About a decade ago:** Michigan State Board of Education, Office of Sex Equity in Education, 1991.

103   **"Boys and girls":** Kimmel, board presentation, *op. cit.*

103   **As the rapper Eminem:** *ibid.*

103   **"All 28 cases":** *ibid.*

104   **"I am not insane":** Michael S. Kimmel, *The Gendered Society.*

104   **Kimmel tells the story:** Kimmel presentation, *op. cit.*

104   **In the film:** *ibid.*

104   **"afraid to do":** *ibid.*

104   **Secretary of Defense:** *New York Times,* March 19, 2003.

105   **Families and schools:** Michelle Conlin, *Business Week,* May 26, 2003.

105   **(Even then, it doesn't quite work):** U.S. Census Bureau, www.census.gov, 2002.

106   **"pay attention to the employees":** Wellesley study, *op. cit.*

106   **"learning organizations":** Peter M. Senge, *The Fifth Discipline.*

106   **Jim Collins:** Jim Collins, *Good to Great.*

106   **Traditionally, our culture:** Joyce K. Fletcher's "The Paradox of Post Heroic Leadership: Gender, Power and the 'New' Organization," Simmons College School of Management, submitted in 2002 to the organization and management theory division of the Academy of Management, and her book *Disappearing Acts.* Other sources: Buchanan, *op. cit.,* Valian, *op. cit.,* and Heifetz, *op. cit.*

111   **Even the so-called gender gap:** Steven Stark, *op. cit.*

111   **Y chromosome:** Maureen Dowd, *New York Times,* July 11, 2003.

112   **With storm clouds:** *Washington Post,* July 29, 2003.

114   **"Good to great":** Collins, *op. cit.*

114   **role *change:*** Joyce Gelb and Marian Lief Palley, *Women and Public Policies.*

Chapter 7: Culture

119   **Poet Audre Lorde said:** Audre Lorde, *Sister Outsider.*

120   **The bureau issued:** "World War II Guide: Wartime Hollywood," www.digitalhistory.uh.edu.

120 **$236.9 billion:** Bob Coen, Universal McCann-Erickson World-group, 2002, www.mccann.com/insight/bobcoen.html.

120 **83 percent:** Slide presentation by Thomas J. Peters, www.rus-sellbeattie.com, March 25, 2003.

120 **$3 trillion market:** Video by Thomas J. Peters, *Women's Millennium: The $3 Trillion Market.*

120 **"Teen-oriented":** *New York Times,* January 26, 2003.

121 **Political candidates also infiltrate:** The Alliance for Better Campaigns, www.bettercampaigns.org, January 1 to November 7, 2000.

121 **"It is through television":** *Who's Talking* study, the White House Project, 2001.

123 **A South African soap opera:** Rasha Abdulla, "Covering the War Tops ICC Agenda," TBS Archives No. 8, Spring/Summer 2002.

123 *Simplemente Maria: ibid.*

126 **Actress Rosanna Arquette:** *People* magazine, August 25, 2003.

127 **Martha M. Lauzen:** *Boxed In: Women on Screen and Behind the Scenes in the 2001–2002 Prime-Time Season,* San Diego State University.

128 **Haysbert:** Jenelle Riley, *Back Stage* magazine, June 19, 2003.

130 **A Hollywood billboard:** *The Celluloid Ceiling: Behind-the-Scenes and On-Screen Employment of Women in the Top 250 Films of 2002,* Martha M. Lauzen, San Diego State University.

130 **Allison Anders:** Laurie Winer, "Women on the Side," *Los Angeles* magazine, September 2000.

132 **OppenheimerFunds:** *From the Locker Room to the Boardroom: A Study of Sports in the Lives of Women Business Executives,* Massachusetts Mutual Life Insurance Company, 2002.

Chapter 8: The Business of Transformation

137 **"To those who":** Women's Environment and Development Web site, www.wedo.com.

138 **Harry Reasoner:** Emily Barker, "Engendering Change," *American Lawyer,* June 2003.

138   **the big bosses:** American Bar Association, "The Unfinished Agenda: A Report on the Status of Women in the Legal Profession," Commission on Women in the Profession, 2001.

139   **As a result:** The No Glass Ceiling Task Force of the Bar Association of San Francisco.

140   **"a Darwinian":** Liz Perle McKenna, *Why Work Doesn't Work Anymore.*

140   **In the words of:** The Living Church Web page, www. catholic.net.

141   **Even worse:** *The Status of Women in Leadership in Alabama,* www.alabamawomen.org.

142   **As Republican governor:** *New York Times,* September 6, 2003.

145   **Research conducted:** Deborah Marlino and Fiona Wilson, "Teen Girls on Business: Are They Being Empowered?," a study by the Committee of 200 and the Simmons College School of Management, 2003.

145   **a poll:** Panetta Institute, "Institute Poll Shows College Students Turned Off by Politics, Turned On by Other Public Service," 2000.

146   **about seven million:** Number derived from a 2003 study by the Center for Information and Research at the University of Maryland, which says there are 12.1 million women between the ages of eighteen and twenty-four, and that 43 percent of them vote.

148   **Ida B. Wells:** From the Duke University Web site, www.duke.edu.

148   **she returned to the South:** From *Ida B. Wells: A Passion for Justice,* a film by William Greaves, 1989.

Bibliography

Abramowitz, Rachel L. *Is That a Gun in Your Pocket: Women's Experience of Power in Hollywood* (New York: Random House, 2000).

Anderson, Trent and Seppy Basili. *Unofficial Unbiased Insider's Guide to the 328 Most Interesting Colleges* (New York: The Kaplan Company, 2003).

Bailyn, Lotte. *Breaking the Mold: Women, Men, and Time in the New Corporate World* (New York: Free Press, 1993).

Bateson, Mary Catherine. *With a Daughter's Eye: A Memoir of Margaret Mead and Gregory Bateson* (New York: HarperPerennial, 1994).

Bell, Derrick A. *Ethical Ambition: Living a Life of Meaning and Worth* (New York: Bloomsbury, 2002).

Buchanan, Constance H. *Choosing to Lead: Women and the Crisis of American Values* (Boston: Beacon Press, 1996).

Carroll, Sue, ed. *The Impact of Women in Public Office* (Bloomington, Ind.: Indiana University Press, 2001).

Clift, Eleanor and Tom Brazaitis. *Madam President: Shattering the Last Glass Ceiling* (New York: Scribner, 2000).

Clinton, Hillary Rodham. *Living History* (New York: Simon & Schuster, 2003).

Cohen, Allan R. and David F. Bradford. *Influence Without Authority* (New York: John Wiley & Sons, 1991).

Collins, Jim. *Good to Great: Why Some Companies Make the Leap . . . and Others Don't* (New York: HarperBusiness, 2001).

Cook, Blanche Wiesen. *Eleanor Roosevelt: 1884–1933, Vol. 1* (New York: Viking, 1993).

———. *Eleanor Roosevelt: 1933–1938, Vol. 2* (New York: Viking, 1999).

Crittenden, Ann. *The Price of Motherhood: Why the Most Important Job in the World Is Still the Least Valued* (New York: Metropolitan Books, 2001).

Debold, Elizabeth, Marie Wilson and Idelisse Malave. *Mother Daughter Revolution: From Good Girls to Great Women* (New York: Bantam, 1994).

Eagly, Alice H. *Sex Differences in Social Behavior: A Social-Role Interpretation* (Hillsdale, N.J.: L. Erlbaum Associates, 1987).

Evans, Gail. *She Wins, You Win: The Most Important Rule Every Businesswoman Needs to Know* (New York: Penguin, 2003).

Fletcher, Joyce K. *Disappearing Acts: Gender, Power, and Relational Practice at Work* (Cambridge, Mass.: MIT Press, 1999).

Flood, Robert L. *Rethinking the Fifth Discipline: Learning Within the Unknowable* (New York: Routledge, 1999).

Folbre, Nancy. *The Invisible Heart: Economics and Family Values* (New York: The New Press, 2002).

Friedan, Betty. *The Feminine Mystique* (New York: W. W. Norton, 1963).

Gelb, Joyce and Marian Lief Palley. *Women and Public Policies: Reassessing Gender Politics,* 3d ed. (Charlottesville, Va.: University of Virginia Press, 1996).

Gerber, Robin. *Leadership the Eleanor Roosevelt Way: Timeless Strategies from the First Lady of Courage* (New York: Prentice Hall Press, 2002).

Gilligan, Carol. *The Birth of Pleasure* (New York: Knopf, 2002).

Gladwell, Malcolm. *The Tipping Point: How Little Things Can Make a Big Difference* (Boston: Little, Brown, 2000).

Goleman, Daniel. *Emotional Intelligence* (New York: Bantam Books, 1997).

Griffith, Elisabeth. *In Her Own Right: The Life of Elizabeth Cady Stanton* (New York: Oxford University Press, 1985).

Hartman, Mary S., ed. *Talking Leadership: Conversations with Powerful Women* (New Brunswick, N.J.: Rutgers University Press, 1999).

Hawthorne, Nathaniel. *The Scarlet Letter* (New York: Modern Library, 2000, originally published in 1850 by Ticknor and Fields, Boston).

Heifetz, Ronald A. *Leadership Without Easy Answers* (Cambridge, Mass.: Harvard University Press, 1994).

Helgesen, Sally. *The Female Advantage: Women's Ways of Leadership* (New York: Doubleday, 1995).

Hochschild, Arlie Russell, with Anne Machung. *The Second Shift: Working Parents and the Revolution at Home* (New York: Viking, 1989).

Jamieson, Kathleen Hall. *Beyond the Double Bind: Women and Leadership* (New York: Oxford University Press, 1995).

Kanter, Rosabeth Moss. *Men and Women of the Corporation* (New York: Basic Books, 1977).

Kennedy, David M. *Freedom from Fear: The American People in Depression and War, 1929–1945* (New York: Oxford University Press, 1999).

Kimmel, Michael S. *The Gendered Society* (New York: Oxford University Press, 2000).

———. *Manhood in America: A Cultural History* (New York: Free Press, 1996).

Kraditor, Aileen. *The Ideas of the Woman Suffrage Movement* (New York: Anchor Books, 1971).

Landes, Joan B. *Women and the Public Sphere in the Age of the French Revolution* (Ithaca, N.Y.: Cornell University Press, 1988).

Liswood, Laura A. *Women World Leaders: Fifteen Great Politicians Tell Their Stories* (San Francisco: HarperCollins, 1995).

Lorde, Audre. *Sister Outsider: Essays and Speeches* (Trumansburg, N.Y.: Crossing Press, 1984).

McKenna, Liz Perle. *Why Work Doesn't Work Anymore: Women, Work and Identity* (New York: Delacourte Press, 1997).

Mikulski, Barbara: et al. *Nine and Counting: The Women of the Senate* (New York: HarperCollins, 2000).

Moncrief, Gary F., Peverill Squire, and Malcolm E. Jewell. *Who Runs for the Legislature?* (Upper Saddle River, N.J.: Prentice Hall Press, 2001).

Naisbitt, John. *Megatrends: Ten New Directions Transforming Our Lives* (New York: Warner Books, 1986).

Norris, Pippa. *Electoral Engineering: Voting Rules and Political Behavior* (New York: Cambridge University Press, 2003).

O'Connor, Sandra Day. *The Majesty of the Law: Reflections of a Supreme Court Justice,* Craig Joyce, ed. (New York: Random House, 2003).

Peters, Thomas J. and Robert H. Waterman Jr. *In Search of Excellence: Lessons from America's Best Run Companies* (New York: Warner Books, 1984).

Quart, Alissa. *Branded: The Buying and Selling of Teenagers* (Cambridge, Mass.: Perseus Publishing, 2003).

Rhode, Deborah L. *Speaking of Sex: The Denial of Gender Inequality* (Cambridge, Mass.: Harvard University Press, 1997).

Senge, Peter M. *The Fifth Discipline* (New York: Doubleday/Currency, 1994).

Steinem, Gloria. *Revolution from Within* (Boston: Little, Brown, 1992).

Swanson, David L. and Paolo Mancini, ed. *Politics, Media, and Modern Democ-*

racy: An International Study of Innovations in Electoral Campaigning and Their Consequences (Westport, Ct.: Praeger, 1996).

Tocqueville, Alexis de. *Democracy in America,* J. P. Mayer, ed.; George Lawrence, tr. (New York: Perennial Classics, 2000; originally published in 1835).

Valian, Virginia. *Why So Slow?: The Advancement of Women* (Cambridge, Mass.: MIT Press, 1998).

Weeden, Curt. *How Women Can Beat Terrorism* (Mount Pleasant, N.C.: Quadra-foil Press, 2003).

Williams, Joan. *Unbending Gender: Why Family and Work Conflict and What to Do About It* (New York: Oxford University Press, 2000).

Index

Ability and women
    in diplomatic relations,
        12–13, 80–86
    in military, 87–90
    of pregnant women, 74–76
    self-evaluation, 61, 79–80
    and social change, 90–93
    stereotypical views, 75–79
Abolitionists, 44
Abramowitz, Rachel, 126
Abzug, Bella, 55, 137, 170
Ackerman, Val, 157
Act-as-if strategy, 68–70
Activism
    of Eleanor Roosevelt, 26–27
    See also Social change
Adams, Abigail, 30–32
Addams, Jane, 44
Advertising, influence on cul-
    ture, 120–22
Aggression
    and manhood, 103–5
    mean girl concept, 60–61
AIDS, awareness and women,
    90–91
Alabama Women's Initiative,
    141–45
Alabiso, Vin, 169
Albright, Madeleine K., 3, 13,
    14, 80–81
Ambition and women
    act-as-if strategy, 68–70
    ambition, expansion of con-
        cept, 69–70
    college as launching point,
        62–63
    compared to men, 30, 53
    encouragement by other
        women, 66–67
    and family work role, 56–59
    and gender inequality,
        61–64
    hard sell, impact of, 55–56
    masking of ambition, 53–55
    mean girl concept, 60–61
    push from others, necessity
        of, 64–66
Anders, Allison, 130
Anderson, Walter, 169
Annan, Kofi, 13, 85
Anthony, Susan B., 32
Arbus, Loreen, 165

Arquette, Rosanna, 126
Arthur, Bea, 125
Athletics, women in, 132–33
Auster, Ellen, 159
Authenticity and women
    barriers to, 106–9
    compromise and corpora-
        tions, 106–10
    disconnection of, 95–99
    and family, 99
    political parties and gender,
        110–13
    and power gains, xv–xvi
    and private life, 113–15
Authority and women, 33–51
    challenges to, 39–40
    compared to men, 36–37,
        39–42
    expansion of, 44–51
    historical view, 30–32,
        44–45, 49–50
    presentation strategies,
        47–49
    slanted media focus, 35–43
    unacknowledged authority,
        39–43

Baker, Paula M., 112
Ball, Lucille, 123–24
Ballard, Marion, 153
Barad, Jill, 118
Barbie doll, President Barbie,
    xv, 117–19
Barnes, Jackie, 163
Barrett, Colleen, 157
Bateson, Mary Catherine, 59
Bell, Derrick, 63
Bergen, Candice, 125
Bernstein, Allison, 167
Berresford, Susan, 167
Bickford, Jewelle W., 164
Bingham, Darcy, 165
Black, Carole, 126
Black, Cathleen, 70
Boydston, Jeanne, 72
Brain, stress reaction and gen-
    der, 89–90
Braun, Carol Moseley, 4
Brockett, Francesca, 161
Bronznick, Shifra, 51, 161, 169
Buchanan, Constance H., 44,
    167

Bullying
    by boys, 104–5
    by girls, 60–61
Bunch, Charlotte, 13
Burk, Martha, 155
Burroughs, Ann, 169
Bush, George W., image as
    leader, 22, 28
Butler, Susan, 160

Career choice, television/
    movie inspired, 122
Carpenter, Bob, 169
Cavanagh, Teresa L., 160
Center for American Women
    and Politics, 9
Change, 137–49
    on ability level, 80–93
    Alabama Women's Initiative,
        141–45
    on ambition level, 66–70
    on authenticity level,
        106–15
    on authority level, 43–51
    and community, 141–43,
        146–48
    cross-cultural view, 11–16
    on cultural level, 117–18,
        122–25, 129–35
    cultural shift, factors in,
        xiv–xv
    culture as agent of, 119–23
    in legal industry, 138–41
    numbers and change, impor-
        tance of, xiii–xiv, 138,
        149
    problems/solutions, exam-
        ples of, 143–45
    and role expansion, 114–15
    social level. See Activism;
        Social change
    TV programs, women's role,
        134–35
    versus extinction, xvii,
        138–39
Chesler, Ellen, 159
Chisholm, Shirley, 32
Chomsky, Noam, 104
*Choosing to Lead: Women and
    the Crisis of American Values*
    (Buchanan), 167
Clark, Wesley, 37

Clinton, Hillary Rodham
  ambition, price of, 30,
    57–58
  in poll on presidency, 65
Clothing, for image of au-
    thority, 48
Cohen, Abby Joseph, 1
College attendance
  female ambition, launching
    of, 62–63
  gender gap, reasons for, 105
Collins, Jim, 106
Community, and change,
    114–15, 141–43, 146–48
Congressional Women's Cau-
    cus, 10
Cornum, Rhonda, 87
Corporations and women
  and compromised authentic-
    ity, 106–10
  glass ceiling, 2
  law firms, positive changes,
    138–41
Corsi, Ginny, 161
Cosgrove, Tom, 169
Creative Experience (Follett), 7
Crittenden, Ann, 71–73
Culture
  advertising, power of, 120–22
  athletics, women in, 132–33
  and career choice, 122
  as change agent, 119–23
  movie industry, 126, 130–31
  and television programs,
    121–30

Dean, Howard, 37, 113, 121
Debold, Elizabeth, 100–101
DeGeneres, Ellen, 125
DeLauro, Rosa, 39
Democratic Party, female sup-
    port, 111–13
Dernocoeur, Kate, 153
Diplomacy and women,
    12–13, 80–86
  female focus, 80–86
  peacemaking, 12–13, 80–86
  terrorism issue, 84–85
  and United Nations, 85–86
Disappearing Acts (Fletcher),
    108
DiVall, Linda, 13, 169
Dobkin, Barbara, 169
Dole, Elizabeth Hanford
  in poll on presidency, 65–66
  slanted media focus on,
    35–37
Doliva, Lauren M., 163
Duckworth, Connie, 152

Eagly, Alice, 96–97
Edelman, Marian Wright, 117
  in poll on presidency, 65
Emotional intelligence (EQ),
    and men, 8
Eng, Phoebe, 154
English, Diane, 128

Ensler, Eve, 49
Entrepreneurs, women as, 3–4
Estrich, Susan, 53
European Parliament, on equal
    participation in diplo-
    macy, 86
Evans, Gail, 48
Evans, Marsha J., 156, 164

Face credibility problem,
    19–20
Family and women
  and ambition, 56–59
  and gender identity,
    100–101
  girls/mothers connection,
    101–2
  household services, cost of,
    72–73
  as leadership barrier, 23–25
  mommy tax, 73
  motherhood as source of
    power/leadership, 71–74
  parental encouragement and
    women, 99
  power and motherhood in-
    compatibility belief, 76
  pregnancy and women lead-
    ers, 74–76
  second shift, 4, 24
  statistics on women and ca-
    reers, 59
Feinstein, Dianne, in poll on
    presidency, 65–66
Female advantage, 6, 21, 108,
    147
Female Advantage, The (Helge-
    sen), 6, 147
Feminine Mystique, The
    (Friedan), 18
Ferrara, Camille, 160
Ferraro, Geraldine, 2, 35
Fili-Krushel, Patricia, 156
Finnbogadottir, Vigdis, 11
Fiorina, Carleton S. (Carly), 2
Fletcher, Joyce K., 107–8, 167
Follett, Mary Parker, 7–8
Fonda, Jane, 98
Foreign policy, women and
    diplomacy, 12–13, 80–86
Foudy, Julie, 133
France, parity in government,
    14, 63
Franklin, Shirley, 19–20
French, Helen, 168
Friedan, Betty, 18
Fudge, Ann, in poll on presi-
    dency, 65

Gardner, Page, 169
Gelb, Joyce, 114
Gender differences
  degree of, 103
  reactions to stress, 89–90
Gender gap, 110–13
Gender inequality and bias
  on ability of women, 77–79

  on ambition and women,
    61–64
  authority issues, 33–51
  on gender and occupations,
    77–78
  income level. See Income in-
    equality
  mean girl concept, 60–61
  in media political coverage,
    35–43
  and religion, 43–44
  See also Leadership barriers
Gender roles, and family,
    100–101
Gerberding, Joan, 164
Gilligan, Carol, 101, 119
Giuliani, Rudy, 21–22
Glass ceiling, 2
Gould, Sara, 168
Government leaders, women,
    3, 4–5, 11–15
  advantages of, 137
  and ambition, 61–64
  authority, expansion of,
    43–50
  characteristics of, 9–13
  international view, 11–15
  leadership barriers, 17–32
  parity, lack of, xiv, 4–5, 15,
    18–21
  peace building, 12–14
  pipeline theory, 21
  skill building, college years,
    62–64
  slanted media focus, 35–39
  statistics on, 4–5
  unacknowledged authority,
    39–43
  and U.S. presidency, 17, 32,
    64–66, 77–78
Gradin, Anita, 15
Granholm, Jennifer, 46
Great Britain, women in Par-
    liament, 78
Griffith, Elisabeth, 159
Guerrilla Girls, 130

Haines, Staci, 92
Hamm, Mia, 133
Harris, Beatrice, 159
Heffernan, Margaret, 3
Helgesen, Sally, 6, 34, 147
Heroic leader concept,
    106–9
Hobson, Mellody, 39–40,
    55–56
Hopkins, Deborah C., 55
How Women Can Beat Terrorism
    (Weeden), 84–85
Human rights issues, 12, 13
Human security concept,
    83–84
Hunt, Swanee, 1, 13, 81, 83
Hutchison, Kay Bailey, 10, 42

Iceland, homemakers on strike,
    11

Income inequality
  for average income level
    women, 25
  for college graduates, 105
  minimum wage and women,
    4
  for women executives, 4
India, women in village councils, 14, 15
International relations, women
  and diplomacy, 12–13,
  80–86
It's Up to the Women (Roosevelt), 67

Jamieson, Kathleen Hall, 169
Jemison, Dr. Mae C., in poll
  on presidency, 65
Job sharing, 33–34
Johnson, Eddie Bernice, 86
Johnson, Vanessa, 91
Joplin, Janis, 95
Jordan, Barbara, 32
Joyaux, Simone, 153
Jung, Andrea, 1

Kaplan, Marley, 161
Kaptur, Marcy, 42–43
Kennedy, Claudia J., Lt. Col.,
  88, 152, 159
  in poll on presidency, 65–66
Kerry, Teresa Heinz, 83
Kimmel, Michael S., 60–61,
  102–4
King, Billie Jean, 1
King, Denise, 91
Kitchen, Patricia, 5
Klein, Laura Cousin, 89
Kravitz, Lee, 169
Krim, Mathilde, 90
Krusa-Dossin, Mary Ann,
  75–76
Kumari, Ranjana, 14

Lagomasino, Maria Elena, 154
Lake, Celinda, 13, 169
Landrieu, Mary L., 76
Lansing, Sherry, 2
Lauzen, Martha M., 127, 130
Law firms, positive changes in,
  138–41
Laybourne, Geraldine, 89–90,
  151
Lazarus, Shelly, 54
Leadership barriers, 17–32
  ability-related, 74–79
  ambition-related, 53–66
  authenticity-related, 106–9
  authority-related, 29–30,
    33–51
  cultural ideals, xiv, 24–25
  face credibility problem,
    19–20
  gender inequality, 17–32
  heroic leader concept,
    106–9
  media-defined leaders, 27–29

parent-worker image, 23–24
qualities of leaders, unnatu-
  ralness for women, 29–32,
  97, 108
symbolic aspects, 79
television programs, men as
  leaders, 126–30
token positions, xiii
toughness issue, 22
Leadership and men. *See* Men
  and masculinity
Leadership and women
  characteristics of, 6–11,
    73–74, 106, 108–9,
    147–48
  female advantage, 6, 21,
    108, 147–48
  and leadership redefinition,
    23–27, 30
  and motherhood, 72–74, 82
Lee, Barbara, 117
Lee, Nancy, 167–68
Legally Blonde, 28, 68, 131, 134
Legislation, related to women,
  10
Lerner, Helene, 163
Lincoln, Blanche, 35, 112
Lingle, Kathleen M., 162
Liswood, Laura, xvii, 1
Living History (Clinton), 58
Logan, Lakita, 91–92
Lorde, Audre, 119

McCain, John, 36–37
McIntosh, Peggy, 167
Madden, Martha, 164
Madres de Plaza de Mayo, 45
Mahlangu, Gwen, 15
Mandabach, Caryn, 156
Mandel, Ruth B., 13
Mandela, Nelson, 86
"Manifesto of the Ten," 14
Mankiller, Wilma P., 117
  in poll on presidency, 65
Marshall, Penny, 131
Marshall, Ruth Ann, 153
Mathews, Jessica Tuchman,
  83–84
Math and science, ability, con-
  ceptions and gender, 61
Mean girl concept, 60–61
Media
  female authority under-
    mined by, 35–39
  hyperwoman image, 29
  leaders defined by, 27–29
  See also Movies; Television
    programs
Men and masculinity
  ability, overvaluation of, 61
  aggression and manhood,
    103–5
  ambition as virtue, 53–54,
    67
  and authenticity, 100–106
  as authorities/experts,
    36–37, 39–42

gender identity and home,
  100–101
image as fathers, 74, 76
inner female, display of,
  21–22
leadership characteristics of,
  6, 105
masculinity-related language,
  102–3
meanness and power, 60
in politics, statistics on, 62
positive media images, 28,
  36–37, 40–42
Republican Party support,
  111
social-emotional skills and
  boys, 105–6
TV series, men as leaders,
  126–30
victimization as boys, 104
Merck, Friedrike, 163
Mikulski, Barbara, 45–46
Military, women in, 87–90
  and pregnancy, 75–76
  sexual attacks on/harass-
    ment, 88–89
Million Mom March, 45
Minard, Sally, 34
Mintzberg, Henry, 6
Mitchell, Pat, 1, 13, 126,
  135
Mommy tax, 73
Moore, Ann, 109–10
Moore, Mary Tyler, 125
Motherhood
  and peacemaking by
    women, 82
  as source of power/leader-
    ship, 71–74
  See also Family and women
Mothers Against Drunk Dri-
  ving (MADD), 45
Movies
  and career choice, 122
  strong women in, 28–29,
    126
  women employed in indus-
    try, 130–31
Movie stars
  men, political careers, 121
  women, popularity, brevity
    of, 126
Mowlam, Marjorie "Mo,"
  13–14, 33
Mulcahy, Anne M., 2
Murray, Patty, 96
Muther, Catherine, 90–91

Napolitano, Janet, 47
National Congress of Mothers,
  44
Ness, Susan, 162
Networks, importance of, 14,
  48
Neufeld, Beverly, 168
Norton, Eleanor Holmes, 11,
  100

O'Connor, Sandra Day, xiii–xiv, 68
Otis, Kimberly, 51
Overholser, Geneva, 158
Overtime work, men versus women, 22–23
Oxytocin, and stress reaction, 89

Palley, Marian Lief, 114
Park, Jeannie, 157
Pauley, Jane, 2
Peacemaking
  female qualities related to, 82
  human security concept, 83–84
  and women, 12–13, 80–86
  women as UN peacekeepers, 85–86
Pelosi, Nancy, 1, 42, 53–54, 113
Perkins, Frances, 4
Peters, Thomas J., 6–7, 106
Physical appearance
  to communicate authority, 47–49
  hyperwoman image, 29
  media focus on, 35–36
Pigott, Jane D., 160
Pintat, Christine, 14
Pipeline theory, 21, 62
Planned Parenthood, 49–50
Political leadership. See Diplomacy and women; Government leaders, women; Leadership and women
Political parties, gender gap, 110–13
Pollitt, Katha, 24
Posa, Cristina, 81, 83
Power imbalance
  and mean girl concept, 60–61
  See also Leadership barriers
Pregnant, ability to lead while, 74–76
President (U.S.)
  in TV programs, 128–30
  women as, 17, 32, 64–66, 77–78
President Barbie, xv, 117–19
Price of Motherhood, The (Crittenden), 71–73
Pruden, Wesley, 54
Prynne, Hester, 29, 68–69
Puriefoy, Wendy, 169

Quality-of-life issues, 12
Quart, Alissa, 120–21
Quindlen, Anna, 22, 97–98

Ragsdale, Rev. Dr. Katherine Hancock, 162
Religion, and gender inequality, 43–44

Republican Party, male support, 111
Rhode, Deborah L., 18, 22
Rice, Condoleezza, 1, 81
Richards, Ann, 98–99
Rodin, Judith, in poll on presidency, 65
Roosevelt, Eleanor
  activism of, 26–27, 32, 149
  on women supporting women, 67
Rosenfeld, Diane, 153
Roudy, Yvette, 14, 15
Rumsfeld, Donald, 104–5

Salser, Cathy, 158
Sanger, Margaret, 49
Scarlet Letter, The (Hawthorne), 29, 68–69
Schakowsky, Jan, 45
Schall, Ellen, 167
Schoettler, Gail, 38–39
Schroeder, Pat, 76
Searching for Debra Winger, 126
Sebelius, Kathleen, 47
Second shift, 4, 24
Sexual attacks/harassment, on military women, 88–89
Shames, Shauna, 168
She Wins, You Win (Evans), 48
Silajdzic, Haris, 80
Silverstein, Melissa, 168
Simmons, Hildy, 154
Sisulu, Sheila, 15
Smalley, Robin, 122–23
Smeal, Eleanor, 13
Smith, Anna Deavere, 1
Smith, Jane E., 166
Snider, Stacey, 125–26
Snowe, Olympia J., 10
Social change
  and ability of women, 90–93
  historical view, 26–27, 44, 148–49
  issues of importance to women, 10–13, 44–47, 49–50, 90–91
Sorenstam, Annika, 133
South Africa, political participation of women, xiv
Spaulding, Jean G., 156
Steinem, Gloria, 49, 58, 96, 134, 149
Stockman, Jennifer Blei, 162
Stress, reaction, gender differences, 89–90
Suffrage movement, 44
Sweden, political participation of women, 15
Sweeney, Anne, 2
Swift, Jane, 74–75

Talk shows, men as experts on, 40–42

Television programs, 121–30
  advertising, power of, 120–22
  and career choice, 122
  change, women's role, 134–35
  educational value, 122–23
  men and authority, 36–37
  men as experts, talk shows, 40–42
  men as leaders, in TV series, 126–30
  men as writers of, 127–28
  as mirror of culture, 123–25, 128
  women in popular programs, 124–25
Temperance movement, 44
Terrorism
  prevention and women, 84–85
  Senate subcommittees and women, 42
Testosterone, 34–35, 89
Thatcher, Margaret, 130
Thomas, Marlo, 125, 129–30
Tibbetts, Pam, 169–70
Till, Kimberly, 166
Title IX, women in athletics, 132–33
Tocqueville, Alexis de, 25
Toulantis, Marie J., 2
Truth, Sojourner, 32

United Nations, women as peacekeepers, 12–13, 85–86

Valian, Virginia, 79
Vernon, Lillian, 165

Wagner, Jeanette, 163
Walker, Mary L., 88
Walters, Barbara, 1
War, women in military, 87–90
Warglo, Lucita, 87
Weeden, Curt, 84–85
Weiss, Jody, 162
Wells, Ida B., 148–49
Whitman, Christine Todd, in poll on presidency, 65–66
Why So Slow? The Advancement of Women (Valian), 79
Williams, Joan, 152
Woodroofe, Natalie, 92
Woodruff, Judy, 13, 165

Yastine, Barbara, 107–8
Yeates, Marie, 138
York, Myrth, 38
Yu, Diane, 155

Zaharias, Babe Didrikson, 133
Zimmerman, Debra, 130